"John Lennon's memorial in Central Park is inscribed with the single word, *Imagine*. This little book has more big ideas and does more to get the church to 'imagine' than most books 5 or 6 times its size. A real gem."
—**Leonard Sweet,** Drew Theological School, George Fox University, preachingplus.com

"Mark Miller has many gifts: an eye for what's worth saying, a knack for saying it clearly and memorably, and enthusiasm that will keep you reading until the last page. And unlike many books that make their point early and then ramble on, this one picks up speed with each chapter, starting strong and saving the best for last. If you want to learn to speak the language of the emerging culture, let Mark be your mentor."
—**Brian D. McLaren,** pastor (crcc.org), author (anewkindofchristian.org), and fellow in emergent (emergentvillage.com)

"For more than four millennia, God's people have been sitting around campfires, in synagogues, and in churches, telling the story of God and God's people. Mark Miller is onto something here: combining that great tradition of telling God's story with new ways of bringing people into that experience. Read this book and know that centuries from now hundreds and thousands of believers will have come to face to face with God through experiential storytelling."
—**Tony Jones,** author, *Soul Shaper: Exploring Spirituality and Contemplative Practices in Youth Ministry* and *Postmodern Youth Ministry: Exploring Cultural Shift, Creating Holistic Connections, Cultivating Authentic Community* (Youth Specialties)

"Mark has performed a noteworthy task...functionally applying postmodern thought to the drive of the church to make the message more creative, meaningful, and experiential. His talent as a practitioner gives him the ability to make each idea and concept immensely practical, not just theoretical. This book belongs on your desk...not stuffed in your bookshelf. You will reference this often."
—**Kevin Salkil,** associate pastor at First Christian Assembly in Cincinnati, Ohio. He also leads a ministry to postmoderns (www.fcacincinnati.org).

"Mark Miller is the real deal. He's a tour guide, a cultural native, who will take you on a journey of discovery, offering the chance to experience communication forms that can make sense of the gospel in post-Christian times."
—**Earl Creps,** Ph.D., D.Min., Director, Doctor of Ministry Program, Associate Professor of Leadership and Spiritual Renewal, Assemblies of God Theological Seminary

"I've utilized Mark's concepts in a postmodern setting with great response. If you intend on communicating effectively in this emerging culture, implement the concepts of *Experiential Storytelling* and watch a generation's thirst for ultimate Truth be quenched."
—**Curt Hughes,** lead pastor of LifeChurch, Wheaton, Illinois (www.getalifechurch.com)

EXPERIENTIAL
STORYTELLING
(Re)Discovering Narrative to Communicate God's Message

Mark Miller

emergentYS Books, 300 South Pierce Street, El Cajon, CA 92020, are published by
Zondervan, 5300 Patterson Aveune SE, Grand Rapids, MI 49530.

Library of Congress Cataloging-in-Publication Data

Miller, Mark, 1968-
   Experiential storytelling : (re)discovering narrative to communicate
God's message / by Mark Miller.
       p. cm.
   ISBN 0-310-25514-7 (pbk.)
   1. Preaching. 2. Storytelling--Religious aspects--Christianity. I.
Title.
   BV4235.S76M55 2004
   251--dc22

                                                                2003015958

Edited by David Sanford
Interior and cover design by Electricurrent
Printed in the United States of America

---

05 06 07 / DC / 10 9 8 7 6 5 4

This book is dedicated to
Stacey, Raegan, and Ramsay.

Table of Contents

During a Jesus Journey...

Just prior to Free Time, a guide announces with a dead-pan face that a terrible disease has been making its way through the camp. He says that it affects people in different ways. A bowl is passed around and the guide tells the teens that whatever affliction was in that bowl has now struck them. Some teens are struck blind (using blindfolds), some lose the use of one arm or leg (using rope), and some are declared "unclean" (using signs). Those who are unclean cannot come with fifteen feet of anyone (unless that other person also is unclean). They also must yell "unclean" wherever they go.

The guide explains there is no cure for this mysterious disease. They are told, however, that a rumor has been going around about a man with a red blanket draped over his shoulder who has the power to heal.

It's interesting to watch the teens form communities based on their afflictions. The "lucky" ones with only an arm affliction occupy their time trying to find the man with the red blanket. This exercise goes on for about an hour. Finally, at long last, the Jesus figure steps onto the scene.

I recall the first time we did this. A teen is sitting on the floor with a blindfold over his head. He is rocking back and forth, very much into the part. The Jesus figure enters the room with the red blanket that had been under the candle during the second Journey. In perfect King James English, this Jesus person (who is unscripted) walks up to the blindfolded teen and says, "What troubles you, my son?"

The teen says, "I am blind, but I was told there was someone with a red blanket with the power to heal me."

The Jesus person replies, "Your faith has made you well." He takes off the teen's blindfold and sternly warns him, "Now do not tell anyone else about this."

Without hesitating, the teen runs upstairs shouting, "I'm healed, I'm healed!"

A swarm of young people suddenly rushes downstairs and through the back door after the man with the red blanket. Some teens lead their blind friends. Others carry the crippled.

Nothing prepared me for this next moment. The "mob" finally catches up with the Jesus person and gathers around him. One by one he touches them and removes whatever troubles them. As the signs, ropes, and blind-folds come off, the teens begin to jump up and down for joy. The Jesus person then walks into the midst of the "unclean" group and heals them.

The gospel has come to life for everyone involved.

Why Experiential Storytelling?

This is a book born from experience and written out of frustration. As I write this, I am sitting next to two women at a Starbucks® who are discussing how one of them has "lost" her brother to Christianity. It is obvious they have no genuine concept of Jesus or the Church. To them, all this Jesus stuff is a "major red flag."

I wish that these women were atypical of the attitudes of most Americans today. The reality is that while America is still the most religious industrialized country in the world, Christianity increasingly is losing its influence. This bothers me! A few years ago the Church's decline hit me hard, and I came to the conclusion that I had only three options. I could sit back and watch it happen. I could take the more popular route of pointing out what was wrong with everyone else. Or I could dive in and, with God's help, do my small part. This book is one result of that third option.

While there are many reasons why the Church in America is in decline, the most striking reason is that people are no longer connecting with the redemptive story of the Bible. We live in a culture that is craving narratives, metaphors, and images—anything that can provide some meaning to their nihilistic lives. The Church has the greatest story ever told. That story, Scripture tells us, is the power of God to transform lives. Yet few are listening. What is wrong with this picture?

I desire for the Church to recapture its ability to converse with culture. I long for American Christians to be able to tell the timeless biblical narrative in the language of the times. This need will not be met by simply reading a book and applying a "how-to" strategy. While there is a "how-to" frequency to this book, I have also tried to transmit on a "why" frequency that I hope you tune in to. This "why" frequency seeks to challenge assumptions and push (insert your church's name here) to unlearn the language of the Church in storytelling and begin to speak a new language.

Several years ago I discovered that my own language was outdated. This realization sent me on a mission to become bilingual and speak the language of our culture. What stemmed from that time was a form of communicating that I call *Experiential Storytelling*.

ex·pe|ri·en·tial sto_|ry·tell′ing
—creating an environment that allows others to participate in the telling of a story through sensory interaction.

My prayer and hope is that the best days of the church lay ahead. If that is going to be true, change is not an option. If this book adds some spice to God's recipe for change, then my mission has been accomplished.

Before we journey together, there are several people I want to thank for making this book possible.

First, I want to thank my family for putting up with my early mornings and late nights. Stacey, my beautiful bride—you are my encouragement, my inspiration, and my love. My precious daughters, Raegan and Ramsay—you are my miracles from God who teach me daily about his wonders. You three are my story, and every day I cannot wait to wake up to what joy you will write on the tablet of my day. I love you beyond what ink will allow me to write. This book is dedicated to each of you.

I also want to thank my father, Clyde Miller, who taught me to work hard and play hard and that "Millers never quit." I want to thank my mom, Anita Miller, for instilling confidence in me that I could do anything. On the days I doubt that, some little voice from my childhood tells me otherwise. It is an inexplicable comfort to know that every morning you are on your knees praying for me. Thanks to my sisters, Debra and Crystal, you have and continue to be two of my best cheerleaders. And I also want to thank my in-laws (or as they would have me say, "in-loves"), Bobby and Sheryl. They continue to show me what a true pioneer spirit looks like. And thanks to their son, my brother-in-law, Chris Beard, you continue to sharpen me and make me want to be a better person.

I want to thank my church, NewSong Church in Cleveland, Ohio. Our pastor, Randy Young, literally said "go for it" to a crazy idea half a dozen years ago that eventually gave birth to this book. Thank you for saying "yes" to innovation in the Church.

In 1998 I attended an event hosted by Leadership Network that took a lot of ideas, assumptions, and jumbled thoughts and connected the dots for me. I was introduced to many people who have and continue to influence me today. Brian McLaren, Stanley Grenz, Leonard Sweet, Sally Morgenthaler, Doug Pagitt, Brad Cecil, Tony Jones, and Andrew Jones were a few of the people I met who planted the seeds of inspiration in my mind and spirit.

There have been many streams of inspiration and influence that have been poured into me by others I have met on the journey since that time. Mark Scandrette, Rudy Carrasco, Spencer Burke, Dieter Zander, Randy Bohlender, Chris Lewis, Rick Commisso, Randy Tomko, Dave Buehring, David Shirk, Steve Fry, Bill Wade, Zach Churchill, Ryan Lott, Gil Dukeman, my profs and friends at Evangel University, and the Journey leadership team all have sown into my life and have helped to shape me. For some of these people, it has been a few intense conversations that changed me. And for others, it is lifelong friendship, mentorship, and community that to me is the stuff of life. All are held in the highest esteem and I want to thank them for their investment.

Finally, I want to thank a couple of men who have had direct input into the development of *Experiential Storytelling*. Mike Gustafson was part of the original design team and pushed me to explore experiential learning. Kevin Salkil is creativity on steroids and his influence on me and this book is profound. Thank you—especially for your friendship.

I hope you enjoy this book.

Mark Miller

CHAPTER ONE

THE DAWNING OF
THE AGE
OF EXPERIENCE

I was eating lunch recently with a friend of mine who is in youth ministry. After the typical small talk and a couple of appetizers, he got unusually quiet. Setting his fork down on his plate, he wiped his mouth and confessed to me, "Nothing works anymore. Everything I was taught about effectively communicating God's Word doesn't work like it used to. Today's teens just don't learn in the same ways. I need help."

Where did you go, Joe DiMaggio?

My sympathies are with my friend. He has stumbled upon a reality that is all too painful for the average minister. We are undergoing one of those important transition times that changes all of the rules.

I began working in full-time ministry more than a decade ago, so I can still recall the days when it was generally accepted that the person behind the podium had something very important to say. So important, in fact, that most people would sit patiently through point after point until those heavily anticipated words "in closing" or "let's bow our heads to pray" were uttered.

Those days have passed. The first day this realization hit me was one of my more unpleasant moments in ministry. I was preaching my Truth from the perch of the platform where the view is normally pleasing. Not this night.

I was on my second of four points on dating when I had a sort of out-of-body experience. Although I was still speaking, I felt like everything coming out of my mouth had that Charlie Brown's teacher sound (wa wa wa wa wa). And peering over the audience, there was a thick glaze beginning to coat the crowd's eyes. They were being hypnotized: getting sleepy, sleepy, sleepy...

What was worse? I was beginning to fall asleep!

I was dying up there—a very slow and painful death. It wasn't for lack of good material. It wasn't for lack of poignant illustrations. And it wasn't for lack of effort. The problem was a disconnect on a grand scale. The disconnect wasn't necessarily the fault of the messenger. Instead, the disconnect revealed a massive systemic dysfunction that has plenty of history, tradition, and baggage. Welcome to the postmodern world.

> **Experience is never limited, and it is never complete; it is an immense sensibility, a kind of huge spider-web of the finest silken threads suspended in the chamber of consciousness, and catching every air-borne particle in its tissue.**
>
> **Henry James**

In many circles the term "postmodernity" has already run its course. Whether or not the term itself has much of a half-life, its cultural effects will be felt for a long time to come.

Postmodernity is one of the most significant cultural changes in the past several centuries. It describes a transitionary time period in which our way of knowing and understanding our world has shifted, leading to significant changes in education and communication.

During the age of modernity, our understanding of the world came from evidence collected through facts. These days of Enlightenment exalted human reason to the throne of understanding. Those in authority became "scientists." Everything was studied under a microscope, including God. Truth was "discovered" and distributed to the masses. New discoveries in technology advanced the modern agenda. One of these, the printing press, created a love affair with the printed word. Combined with a love of reason, the importance of the mystery, stories, and personal life experiences diminished. Each had been valued components in premodern times.

In the highly individualistic climate of modernity, reactions started to occur. People felt force-fed a plate of cold, hard facts. Questions surfaced about how reliable those facts actually were. Meanwhile, technological advances eventually allowed for the possibility of choice, blurring the lines of reality in the process. Radio, television, computers, and finally the Internet created an entirely new world. Old techniques were increasingly met with a "been there, done that" attitude.

People want interaction, something that will jar them out of their monotony. They want to be touched, not by the numbing effect of a top-down monologue aimed at the mind, but by the power of a full-bodied personal experience.

ex•pe•ri•ence :
the apprehension of an object, thought, or emotion through the senses or mind; an event or a series of events participated in personally.

Experience rules

This is the world in which we now live. Experience is the new king of the mountain. There are no passive participants. Missing the effects of this experiential renaissance from the home to the classroom to business is impossible. Take your local restaurant. Have you noticed that the kitchens are more open, allowing you to see the chefs prepare your food while you sip your drink and converse with your friend?

Several years ago the national restaurant chain Mongolian Barbecue© put a new spin on the old-fashioned buffet idea, even letting you come up with the recipe for your original creation. They provide the ingredients; you choose which ones you want in your bowl. Spice it up the way you like it and they cook it in front of your eyes. If you're bored watching the cooks prepare your meal, you can play one of the vintage games at the counter. You may or may not leave with a great taste in your mouth, but you will definitely leave with a fun experience that has engaged more than your taste buds.

> ## Not the fruit of experience but experience itself, is the end.
>
> ## Walter Pater

A few years ago would you have paid more than a dollar for a cup of coffee? Now you walk into a coffeehouse where you hear cool music, watch the coffee-bar attendants make your drink, perhaps relax on one of the hip pieces of furniture, and think that a $3 cup of coffee is a bargain. Why? Because you bought more than coffee—you paid for an experience. It's caffeine for the senses.

Even local department stores and grocery stores are becoming experiential. My wife and I recently registered for our second baby shower. A few years ago, registering for our first baby shower was a painful experience (at least for me). I sat motionless in the "men's chair" while Stacey filled out page after page of product information. Now, I simply typed in our name at a computer, took a scanner in hand (I pretended it was a laser gun), and began beaming our wish lists into the computer.

The only kind of learning which significantly influences behavior is self-discovered or self-appropriated learning—truth that has been assimilated in experience.

Carl Rogers

While some states have had this concept for years, the rest of the country is learning what the term "self-scan" means. Rather than stand passively watching someone scan your food items for you, you now have the chance to do it yourself. You scan it, you pay for it, and you bag it. Part of the appeal is expediency, but another appeal is the opportunity for active participation. It's fun to do it yourself.

My daughter has enough stuffed animals to fill a small zoo. Not too long ago we had "the talk." I told her that it was time for our zoo to stop taking in any more animals. Having reluctantly agreed, she then proceeded to talk us into buying another stuffed teddy bear. This was not any ordinary bear, however...this was a Build-a-Bear®. A Build-a-Bear is a toy animal you stuff and dress yourself. Before your eyes, you fill this little lifeless shell of fur with a figurative breath of life. You leave $30 poorer, but how often have you participated in the birth of a stuffed animal?

You cannot create experience. You must undergo it.

Albert Camus

Entertainment is also exploring new territories. In their book *The Experience Economy*, Joseph Pine and James Gilmore say that "entertainment provides not only one of the oldest forms of experience, but also one of the most developed and, today, the most commonplace and familiar." The industry realizes that the audience is no longer content to simply window-shop. The reality shows of the past few years have allowed us to jump into the screen and become a part of television. Millions of viewers watch week after week anticipating—indeed, looking forward to—the troubles and conflicts of the cast. We then gather around the water cooler at work to discuss who has been voted off what show. Each viewer believes "I could do that." Many shows now link with Web sites, giving viewers an additional interactive experience.

Theatre experiments like Blue Man Group have taken the idea of experiential theatre to another level. The show itself is one great experience, but no need to wait for the show to start for your experience to begin. While waiting in line, a variety of entertaining distractions prevent boredom. Words and images flash above you and PVC pipes suddenly appear, transporting voices from an unknown source on the other end. Waiting in line has never been so much fun! During the show, you might be showered with "debris" from their creations or brought up on stage to become a human paintbrush. This group crosses all traditional boundaries, ensuring that every space and every moment is immersed in experience. You have no choice but to be touched by the show.

There is no doubt that all our knowledge begins with experience.

Immanuel Kant

My hometown of Cleveland, Ohio, has a long history of theatre. It is home to the second largest theatre district in the United States. One of the shows made the news after setting a new record as the longest running show in Cleveland history. The show is *Tony and Tina's Wedding*, which has played in many other cities as well. The audience comes to the performance with an invitation to the wedding. While watching the wedding and dining at the reception, audience members may unwittingly become characters in the unfolding comedy. Each evening the audience becomes an integral part of the storyline.

What I hear, I forget.
What I see, I remember.
What I do, I understand.

Kung Fu Tzu (Confucius)

The electronic gaming industry is the real leader in experiential entertainment. With light-speed technological advances, this industry has sales that more than double that of the multi-billion-dollar-a-year movie industry. Microsoft®, the most profitable company in the history of the world, bet the farm that the gaming industry is where the money is with its Xbox™ system. It is not enough to simply watch and interact with the screen; Controllers now "shock" your hands as you play the game.

In business, understanding the difference between the old language of *information* and the new language of *experience* is critical. Ignorance can cost you your audience—and a lot of money.

One example of those who "get it" and those who do not can be found in the comparison of the Rock and Roll Hall of Fame Museum in Cleveland and the Music Experience in Seattle. The Hall features a walk of fame displaying the names of musical icons voted into the Hall of Fame. It does an adequate job of allowing you to view costumes, memorabilia, and pieces of history.

> **The things we know best are the things we haven't been taught.**
>
> **Marquis de Luc Vauvenargues, French moralist**

The Music Experience, on the other hand, is a sensory explosion. People navigate the museum with a PDA that, when aimed at a display, provides immediate interaction. To hear the guitar you are staring at play the music it has produced, one simply aims, clicks, and listens. In the play area, everyone becomes a rock star. Anyone can walk into a soundproof cubicle and play music at decibels that can make your ears bleed. There is even a music video simulator.

Not surprisingly, the Music Experience is breaking new records in attendance while the Rock Hall is considering reducing the number of operating hours.

"E" is for experience

The age of experience has had a dramatic effect upon education. Have you ever participated in a team-building exercise? How about creative problem-solving exercises or maybe ropes course training? All these methods of learning are part of a growing educational philosophy called "experiential education."

There can be no knowledge without emotion. We may be aware of a truth, yet until we have felt its force, it is not ours. To the cognition of the brain must be added the experience of the soul.

Arnold Bennett, British novelist

Proponents of experiential education critique the traditional classroom style with its hierarchal structure. They see traditional education style as a deductive approach that begins with an assumption that an information transfer must occur between enlightened teacher to ignorant student (sound familiar?). This style of a classroom will have row upon row of chairs facing the educator and his or her blackboard.

Today's emerging generations no longer need the informed to be the informer. The Internet has given them unprecedented access to information that's only a few clicks away. This shift in need has also brought a shift in learning styles. Experience that is interactive and relational not only attracts the younger generations, but is the key to educating them as well.

The real beauty of experiential education is that it places trust in the learner to derive meaning from his or her experience. As a learning environment is created, the active focus shifts from the educator to the student. This interactive approach actively involves the learner in a more holistic and integrated educational process. It assumes that people are created differently and that each possesses an individual learning style.

Meanwhile, back in Mayberry

Obviously, society has been greatly impacted by the seismic changes in culture and technology. During this time the Church has not had a Teflon® coating that somehow has protected it from the effects of culture. Instead, the Church has been a willing participant in the age of modernity.

> ### The art of teaching is the art of assisting discovery.
>
> ### Mark Van Doren, poet

While there have been some moves toward more contemporary worship services, the teaching and educating of the flock has remained largely unchanged for centuries. Forward-facing seating, the lectern (pulpit), the three-point messages—outlined in the form of an alliteration, of course—have become sacred relics. In many cases, those relics have worn out their welcome.

Educators and entertainers have found experience to be an increasingly important part of the process, but many in the Church fear that any turn toward the experiential is negative. One fear is that the Word of God is somehow cheapened by the primacy of experience. While we obviously must continue to handle God's Word cautiously, we must remember that the Church throughout the centuries has repeatedly contextualized its message in an understandable language. We can look to the great reformers, Bible translators, missionaries, and others throughout history who have been champions at this.

> **Truth divorced from experience will always dwell in the realms of doubt.**
>
> **Henry Drause**

Today's Church leaders must see themselves as missionaries who are setting sail from the land of modernity to the uncharted waters of postmodernity. And the first rule for any missionary is to understand the language and culture of his or her community.

Experience is one of the primary languages of postmodern culture. This has vast implications for the Church. Spiritually, it means that people are more open and ready than ever to experience the mystery and awesome power of God. In the practice of ministry, however, it means nothing less than a complete reconstruction of how we communicate and educate.

The Church is in the communication business. We have the most profound story of all time and yet we are lulling today's generations to sleep. My "out-of-body" experience mentioned earlier in this chapter was my catalyst for dreaming what ministry could look like in this postmodern world.

What if we were to take our message and begin speaking the language of the natives? Instead of telling people Jesus is the light of the world, what if we showed them the stark difference between light and darkness?

What if we removed all of the argumentative language, replaced it with beautiful narratives, and let people feel the power of story? Instead of trying to convince people to accept a list of spiritual laws, how about placing individuals in the story, allowing them to learn and interact with God's character?

What if we told our story in a holistic manner engaging all of the God-given senses?

What if...?

CHAPTER TWO

ONCE UPON A STORY

Truth, naked and cold, had been turned away from every door in the village. Her nakedness frightened the people. When Parable found her, she was huddled in a corner, shivering and hungry. Taking pity on her, Parable gathered her up and took her home. There, she dressed Truth in story, warmed her and sent her out again. Clothed in story, Truth knocked again at the villagers' doors and was readily welcomed into the people's houses. They invited her to eat at their table and warm herself by their fire.

Jewish teaching story

It is impossible not to notice the storytelling renaissance. Society is rediscovering the subtle power and beauty of story. And storytelling is everywhere. It is king in today's world of communication.

From business to Hollywood, from the classroom to the living room, story is as much a part of everyday life now as the latest technology. Talk shows tell stories. Commercials tell stories. Magazines tell stories. One of the most popular magazines claims "Every life has a story."

Even the daily news is no longer news unless it is a story. In a recent commercial, a news anchor for CNN said: "It's not enough to have a great story—we have to be great storytellers."

sto_|ry·tell´er:

a person who invites others to enter into the experience of a story.

In my hometown of Cleveland, the Indians baseball team is currently in a rebuilding phase. Rebuilding is a code word for "our team stinks but just wait till next year." This basically means that you pay the same amount of money as when they had a good team. So how do they choose to sell tickets? Free giveaways? More novelty nights with fireworks or other entertainment? No.

Instead, they have been bombarding the airways with commercials telling the stories of each of their "unknown" players. They've told the story of an immigrant from Latin America, for instance, and the story of an underdog overachiever who spent nine years in the minor leagues before making it to the majors. The management hopes that, despite the team's win-loss record, people will be moved by the stories of these teammates.

Storytelling has been around since the beginning of human history. Story by definition is a telling or retelling of something. Most definitions include the word "verbal." I believe that is too limiting. Some of the most powerful stories told today use very few words. They also do not require much time. I am still surprised at how a thirty-second commercial without spoken words can move me to tears.

The history of story

Most educators trace ancient storytelling to the bards. A bard was a poet whose duty was to compose poetry and narration to retell the exploits and praise the heroic deeds of various tribal leaders. He used story, poetry, music, and other art forms to communicate his message.

Other ancient storytelling forms can be found in caves with symbols written on the wall to tell the tales of war and adventure. Some of those symbols also told about mundane life events like chores and caring for families. Storytelling became the vehicle to pass on the history and traditions of one generation to the next.

The disciples came to him [Jesus] and asked, "Why do you speak to the people in parables?" He [answered:] "This is why I speak to them in parables: "Though seeing, they do not see; though hearing, they do not hear or understand. In them is fulfilled the prophecy of Isaiah: " 'You will be ever hearing but never understanding; you will be ever seeing but never perceiving. For this people's heart has become calloused; they hardly hear with their ears, and they have closed their eyes. Otherwise they might see with their eyes, hear with their ears, understand with their hearts and turn, and I would heal them.' "

Jesus (Matthew 13:10-15)

Story has been around so long because God created humanity with the capacity to interpret its surroundings.

We were created with a curiosity, a complexity, and a need for meaning. That longing to understand the bigger questions is a deep need that cannot be filled with mere facts. God did not choose to reveal a list of facts to us. The Old Testament was given to humanity in the form of narratives and poetry. Even the writing of the law took place in the midst of the deeply compelling story of God redeeming his chosen people.

The influence of story

Storytelling is powerful because it has the ability to touch human beings at the most personal level. While facts are viewed from the lens of a microscope, stories are viewed from the lens of the soul. Stories address us on every level. They speak to the mind, the body, the emotions, the spirit, and the will. In a story a person can identify with situations he or she has never been in. The individual's imagination is unlocked to dream what was previously unimaginable.

Early in our ministry, my wife and I pioneered a new ministry geared toward emerging adults. The group started with about ten or fifteen eager young people curious to see what this new ministry was all about. Being new at this, we did what we knew to do: open in prayer, share some announcements, and then proceed to lead a book study for the next 45 minutes. Everything went very well for the first two weeks. Then slowly, one by one, the exodus began. Before long the class consisted of my wife, me, and a loud cricket in the corner of the room.

> **An artist like me gets out of his work exactly what he puts into it. If you're really interested in the characters you're drawing—if you truly understand and love them—then the people who look at your sketches will feel the same way about them.**
>
> **Norman Rockwell**

Something was not connecting with this group of young people—and everything was pointing in our direction! After spending several weeks in prayer, and asking for counsel from the one or two remaining participants (cricket included), we realized that the one missing component in this ministry was an opportunity for relational connections to happen. One way we set out to solve the problem came in the form of telling stories. These stories came not from the teachers but from the students. They began to tell their stories—and the positive response to this decision was immediate.

A single mom told the first story. She had turned away from God and one day found out she was pregnant. She told us how she agonized over whether she should keep the child. She also described a past where men had brought her much pain. From that abuse this woman had built up emotional barriers designed to keep out anything that hinted of goodness. During a moment of intense soul-searching, however, she felt the hand of God upon her. It was not the cold hand she expected, but instead the warm, caring touch from a heavenly Father who drew her into his safe embrace. That one moment melted all of the icy barriers built up around her heart. She soon experienced the blessing of forgiveness that had eluded her for so long.

> **Facts cannot speak for themselves. Facts are dependent upon context. Context is everything.**
>
> **Annette Simmons**

Everyone in the room sat in awe at the power of this single mom's story. One by one they came up to encourage and comfort her. Several told her, "I never knew."

More and more stories were shared. Within a few Sundays, the room where we met filled back up. Before long, we set up chairs outside of the room so more people could listen in to what was going on. In addition, that single mom and my wife started a new ministry for young single moms, many of whom had similar stories of a painful past.

> Stories are "more true" than facts because stories are multi-dimensional. Truth with a capital "T" has many layers. Truths like justice or integrity are too complex to be expressed in a law, a statistic, or a fact. Facts need the context of when, who, and where to become Truths.
>
> **Annette Simmons**

The grand disconnect

Today's postmoderns are extremely receptive to stories. This is due in part to the collapse of the grand story in Western society. For centuries almost everyone was connected to the same story, and each person had the same beginning to his or her story: "In the beginning God created..." This story defined people's lives. It created a comfort and safety, a type of glue that held everything together.

In postmodernism, however, every story is equally valid and anyone who would impose his or her story as the only story is written off as an intolerant simpleton. This poses a grave challenge to those who try to preach absolute truth. An increasing number of people are asking, *Whose truth?*"

> **God knew what He was doing when He chose story, narrative as a primary way to reveal Himself to us.**
>
> **Dr. Daniel Taylor, in an interview with Kathi Allen**

Without uttering a word, the average audience in America today comes to a church gathering with negative assumptions and a measure of skepticism. This prevailing attitude is yet another reason why story is such a natural connecting point for the church and culture. People can argue doctrine and theology. They can even sit with arms crossed listening to someone's convincing reasons why they should believe. But when powerful stories begin to be told, and when a person can identify with another person's journey, the arms drop, the defensiveness wanes, and a receptive ear is gained. Faith has become personal.

We live in an increasingly complex society. Stories connect with people today precisely because they acknowledge the realities of everyday life. In her book *The Story Factor*, Annette Simmons says, "Story can hold the complexities of conflict and paradox."

At the end of a modern equation, all the facts must add up. Two plus two must always equal four. While we want things to add up, the reality is that a lot of things in life do not add up precisely or logically. By definition, science effectively removes the most human aspect of being alive—our relational connections. And yet this is precisely where the longing in the human heart begins, in a longing for relational connections. Life is messy and no one understands that more than today's seekers. Nice, neat, prepackaged messages do not address the human condition like they once did.

Sadly, for quite some time the church has been under the assumption that everyone still gets the story. The average church leader still thinks, "What they need are facts—evidence that will compel them to change." They have bought into the old Enlightenment idea that salvation is an equation.

In the words of Annette Simmons:

Story is your path to creating faith.... People value their own conclusions more highly than yours. They will only have faith in a story that has become real for them personally. Once people make your story, their story, you have tapped into the powerful force of faith.

The great storyteller

The irony of the Church's modern predicament is that Jesus used stories all the time. In fact, the apostle Matthew tells us, "Jesus spoke all these things to the crowd in parables; he did not say anything to them without using a parable" (Matthew 13:34) *New Living Translation*. These parables were not good illustrations to punctuate his points. The stories themselves revealed the hidden mysteries of God.

> Stories are able "to integrate the transcendent and the immanent, the sacred and the profane."
>
> **Ronald Sider and Michael Ling**

What we usually do not see in the text of the Gospels, of course, is the dialogue Jesus is having with his audience while telling each story. What we do see with humorous frequency is the disciples scratching their heads. While

Jesus did explain many of his parables, there is scant evidence that he tied everything up into nice, neat packages. He could have said, "Okay, listen; let me break it all down for you. Here are four steps to conversion" or "five things to lead to a stress-free life." He then could have proceeded to give everyone the answers for everything. He could have gained the undisputed title of the World's Best Answer Man. Jesus also could have opened the Hebrew texts, read every passage flawlessly, exegeted every paragraph with precision, and explained every verse in minute detail.

> **The Fantastic or Mythical is a Mode [that] has the same power: to generalize while remaining concrete, to present in palpable form not concepts or even experiences but whole classes of experience, and to throw off irrelevancies. But at its best it can do more; it can give us experiences we have never had and thus, instead of 'commenting on life', can add to it.**
>
> **C.S. Lewis**

But he chose not to do any of that. Instead, he chose to tell stories. He told stories based on the experiences of the people. He told stories of things people had never thought of. He told stories that caused people to think. These provocative tales made his audience wrestle to understand what he meant. A Samaritan is a hero? A king extends invitations to commoners? And what is this with a landlord who doesn't seem to mind killing one of his servants? These are not trim, tidy, well-edited messages. They are raw stories aimed at the heart by way of the ear.

A sermon tells people what to think. A story forces people to do the thinking for themselves. It can feel dangerous because it allows for interpretation. But one of the adjectives used to describe the Holy Spirit is "counselor." Do we trust our people and the Holy Spirit enough to allow them to think for themselves? Can we leave something open-ended, knowing the conclusion might not come until later that day, week, month, or year? Can we allow people to own the stories? Or do we do all of the interpreting and leave nothing to the imagination?

My belief is that when a story becomes personal and people begin to become unsettled and challenged by it, then they have been touched in a place where facts fear to tread. It is a place so personal that it can spark an inner transformation.

From good to great stories

The sad reality is that the Church has a great story. No, it has the greatest story. Sadly, for too many today, that story is tired and worn out.

At a time when so few people in Western society are familiar with the biblical story, one would think this would be a prime opportunity for the Church to retell that story—using our God-given imaginations—in order to reconnect people to the power of its message.

After all, people are searching. God has placed in humans a supernatural search engine that has the simple word "meaning" typed in the blank. By nature, every human being keeps hitting the search button. Most of the time that search is in vain. But God wants the Church to be his mouthpiece to point to ultimate meaning. When individuals encounter our story in a way they can understand, they will respond.

Dieter Zander, a church planter in California, compares the effect of this kind of storytelling to the strings of a guitar:

> When you put your face next to an "A" string and begin to hum an "A"—that string will begin to vibrate. The "D" won't, the "G" won't, but the "A" will.

Because it was created to vibrate with that tone. The thing about the story—God's story—is that when it is told and applied well, and when it is supported in a sensorial way, something inside our heart starts to vibrate, regardless of whether we are a Christian or not, because we were created for our hearts to vibrate with that story.

Not just any story can do that. We must tell God's story and tell it well.

Telling a good story takes practice. Telling a great story takes a little more. This book focuses more on the Experiential Storytelling medium than telling stories. As such, I use the term "story" loosely. In Experiential Storytelling, the story could actually be a concept or idea. Although Experiential Storytelling does not require that a story be told word-for-word, the story must be communicated effectively. Even great stories can become average or worse if we're not careful. Here are some guidelines to consider before bringing your story to life.

Know the story

This principle applies whether you are creating a story or retelling one. You must know the story inside and out. If someone were to ask you what the story is about, you need to be able to retell the story and explain it in simple terms.

Remember that the most effective communicators take complex ideas and make them understandable. People might be compelled to think differently by a provocative story, but if they are left more confused than before, you have not done your job.

Work on your story by retelling it to a friend. Then take time to retell the story to yourself. It might seem a little strange, but find a quiet place, close the door, and tell your story. The more you are able to tell or explain your story, the better you will get to know the story. You'll also discover to what extent you know the story at that point.

Wendy...was just slightly disappointed when he admitted that he came to the nursery window not to see her but to listen to stories. "You see, I don't know any stories. None of the lost boys knows any stories." "How perfectly awful," Wendy said.

J.M. Barrie, *Peter Pan*

Know your audience

It's not enough to know your story. You must also know your audience in order to tell the story effectively. What are their limitations? Younger people tend to have shorter attention spans and need more concrete ideas. Older people tend to handle abstractions better and might appreciate more subtleties. If you have an artistic group, you might be able to use representations that you could not get away with in another group. Each group will respond differently to a given story or presentation, so always ask questions about how best to present your story to a given audience.

What language does your audience speak? My in-laws are missionaries in Eastern Europe. Their very first job as missionaries was to learn the language of the people. When they arrived in Austria for missionary training, the first thing they did was enroll in language school. The same rules apply with communicating your story. This missional mind-set places the priority on the hearer, not the teller. Listen with the ears of those who hear you.

There are endless possibilities in telling or retelling stories, just as there are endless subcultures within our culture. I was recently on a missions trip to Uganda. Within this country, the size of the state of Oregon, more than 50 different dialects are spoken. In the eastern inner-rim suburbs of Cleveland, a number of cultural dialects are spoken, as well. Drive five minutes from my house in any given direction and you might as well be in another country. Everyone speaks English, but that is where the similarities end. There is an Italian neighborhood, an inner-city neighborhood, a Jewish neighborhood, an eastern European neighborhood.

Knowing your audience will allow you to present the story in their language. This is especially true in telling stories experientially. With the addition of many different media, it adds another dimension of creativity within your story that will allow you to become even more personal. This is where the real fun begins!

> [Steve] Jobs is a great speaker because he is a great storyteller. If you look at all of his recent presentations, you'll see that he's in fact telling a story each time he gets on the stage. Instead of "Here's the new G5, which is faster and better," he says "Here's how we sat down and thought about how to reinvent the G5 to make it faster and better." …Jobs' storytelling approach really affects the way people think about himself and about Apple.
>
> **Jason Whong's Internet post on Steve Jobs**

Honor thy story

It is easy and sometimes necessary to take artistic license when dealing with an abstract concept in storytelling. Many times, the more creative you are, the more the hearer will experience, and the greater the likelihood that they will remember the story.

Some stories, however, should not be tampered with. This includes but is not limited to biblical stories. Be careful that you do not edit too much so the story loses its integrity. This does not mean that you should not experiment with biblical stories; instead, simply be careful when you do. When in doubt, ask for guidance from someone who has biblical training or to consult a respectable Bible commentary or dictionary. The message you are trying to convey is of much more importance than the methods you employ in telling the story.

Remember that this book is about a desire to tell the timeless story of the Bible to an emerging and changing culture. Methods change, but the message does not. We must preserve the integrity of God's story at all costs.

Ask lots of questions

Asking questions about your story is the key to unlocking creativity. It is also the tool that allows you to see your story from all sides. Here are five sets of core questions to help you understand and tell your story more effectively:

▸ *What is the core message of the story? Is that the same message we want to convey?*

▸ *From whose point of view will this story come? Would the story be any stronger if told from a different point of view? Is any narration needed?*

▸ *What is the setting of the story? Would it be more compelling to use a new setting?*

▸ *What kind of conflict arises in the story? Individual vs. God? Individual vs. Satan? Individual vs. Second Individual? Individual vs. Nature? Individual vs. Society? Individual vs. Himself? Individual vs. Machine? Or God vs. Satan? What are some abstract or contemporary ways we could capture this conflict?*

▸ *What details could we add to enhance the story? What details could we leave out?*

Once you know your story, know your audience, and ask the appropriate questions to broaden your perspective, you're ready to take your story to the next level—adding experience.

CHAPTER THREE

AWAKENING THE SLEEPING GIANT IN THE CHURCH-CREATIVITY

The reason you picked this book may have had something to do with its subtitle—*(Re)Discovering Narrative to Communicate God's Message*. I am tempted to become very pragmatic and skip ahead to what works, letting you take those ideas and cram them into your box, hoping that there is a fit of some sort. This would be a mistake.

Your desire to communicate more effectively is not a church growth strategy; instead, it is a mandate of the Church! God called us to go and make disciples. This begins with relationships and continues when we communicate the Good News. Since we have been entrusted with telling and retelling the greatest story ever told, we must speak the language of an ever-changing culture.

Cutting and pasting good ideas will not produce a better means of communicating. What will raise the bar within the Church is for each of us to realize the creative wealth that is right under our noses. Today, more than ever, the greatest creative impulse is at the community level. Consider what Donald Miller says in his book *Reinventing American Protestantism*:

> The centers of energy and creativity in this decade lie at the local, not the national level... The really innovative ideas for reshaping the church will come from people working in the trenches.

This is a challenge for church leaders to learn the language of the people in their own community and respond with new and fresh ways of communicating. To communicate effectively in our postmodern world, we must have the ability to think creatively and adapt quickly. My desire in this chapter is to stir up the creative spirit within you and give you some ideas on how to do that.

Before we explore the what-ifs, it is worth spending a few paragraphs conjecturing on why the Church is lagging behind culture in the creativity department. For centuries the Church was the center of thought and artistic expression. What happened?

The great divorce

The Church has a storied history of tension between faith and art. Many historical turning points reveal this tension.

The most famous turning point is probably the Reformation. With Johann Gutenberg's invention of the printing press, and Martin Luther's decision to publish his 95 Theses, the written word took precedence in the Protestant Church over other forms of communication. In the name of reform, the Church was stripped of art, image, and anything else that would cause one to be distracted from the reading, preaching, and hearing the Word of God. The Reformers preferred a lecture style. Seats faced forward to receive the Word, eyes were closed during prayers, and the pulpit was placed at the highest point on the platform.

In America, early Christian leaders hitched a ride on the Reform wagon and continued to nix artistic expression for generations. Anything but the pure preaching of the Word was considered a distraction at best. Many thought art had nothing to say about God, the Bible, and the Christian faith. Beyond art, the imagination found itself in the crosshairs of the times. Jonathan Edwards, the great preacher and educator, took aim by saying:

> The imagination or fancy seems to be that wherein are formed all those delusions of Satan, which those are carried away with who are under the influence of false religion and counterfeit graces and affections. Here is the devil's grand lurking place, the very nest of foul and delusive spirits.

Re:form

These intersections in history created an alienation and tension for Christian artists that continues to this day. The Church and the arts, creativity, and imagination have been at war for far too long. It is time to call a truce. No, a surrender. A surrender by the Church (waving the white flag) that accepts that creativity and imagination are gifts from God, not somehow profane. These valuable gifts need nourishment, not further neglect. And they must be exercised both inside and outside the walls of the Church.

The good news: the Church is beginning to welcome back the artist. This is probably due more to survival instincts than reconciliation, but the result is the same. And the language of today's visual culture is aesthetics. A church that wishes to speak that language will embrace the creators of aesthetics. William Dyrness of Fuller seminary says, "Regardless of whether one considers this good or bad, for this generation, aesthetics counts more than epistemology."

Most people die before they are full born. Creativeness means to be born before one dies.

Erich Fromm

This book is *not* about mining new sermon illustrations. This book is about taking a fresh look at the very methods we use to present our life-changing message. This will require an awakening.

Good morning!

It's time to start thinking differently.

In the beginning, God created...

Creativity started long before the first human artist shaped a piece of clay or scribbled on the inside of a cave. God is *the* author of *all* creativity. Genesis begins the grand story of earthly creativity with the truly mind-bending divine act of creation. And in response to the conflict started at the Fall comes the most amazing act of creation. The Creator and Author writes himself into the story and joins his creation!

Every child is an artist. The problem is how to remain an artist once he grows up.

Pablo Picasso

Across his cosmic storyline, God has written in the word "redemption." Now, he invites the church to join him in the redemptive process. I see this redemptive process not through the lens of a scientist with formulas or of a factory worker on an assembly line, but rather through the lens of an artist. Redemption cannot be contained in finite formulas and programs. Instead, redemption begins by viewing the Word through the limitless eyes of an immortal God. This takes an open mind, a willing heart, and a creative spirit. The Holy Sprit guides that process with an unending supply of creative energy (if the Church allows that energy to be accessed).

In the process, we must always remember that God *is* the author of creativity. There is nothing new under the sun. The great Creator has already beaten us to it. Understanding this helps us to start in a humble posture and to direct all honor where it is due, to the glory of God.

Creativity "defined"

In this spirit, I want to offer a few thoughts on creativity. Most of these ideas I have collected over the years by individuals much more creative than I. These individuals probably received them from other people more creative than they. I share these thoughts out of a desire for everyone to know the joy of creating and the fulfillment of bringing to our Creator his rightful praise. Some may say this does not seem very "spiritual." I could not disagree more. When we shed the chains of traditions and assembly-line faith, we open ourselves up to a type of freedom that I see permeating Scripture.

Creativity is the ability to think or act differently. Notice I did not say to think up something new or to create something new. Creativity is just different…even perhaps different only for you. You allow your mind to soar to places it has not been in a long time, if ever.

So, in the spirit of soaring, let's look at the creative process like flying a sleek new airplane. Every ride requires flight preparation, take-off, air time, and landing.

The flight prep

Flight prep is all about a mind-set. It is tough to truly change our mind. The older we are, the more our mind is set. So check the engine of your mind and make sure it's in proper working order before you attempt your creative voyage. Here are a few steps to help you do this.

1. Kid-minded

Jesus told his disciples, "unless you change and become like little children, you will never enter the kingdom of heaven" (Matthew 18:3).

Kids are amazing. I know because I have a nine-year-old named Raegan who amazes me on a daily, sometimes hourly, basis. I have a notebook where I keep my Raegan quotes. When I am acting too old, I pull them out. Here are a few:

"What if we didn't have tongues?"

"Jesus hears you when you're not even talking. He listens to your heart."

> **Man can live without air for a few minutes, without water for about two weeks, without food for about two months—and without a new thought for years on end.**
>
> **Kent Ruth**

"Daddy, I think that Jesus should be white *and* black."

"When we sing, it's just like we're praying to God."

"Is there a different heaven for flowers and trees and animals?"

I usually find it difficult to respond to Raegan's questions and observations. They catch me off guard and I find myself searching for a context. Kids have no need for a neat and tidy context. They also are not challenged by what they have been told they cannot do. Kids do not color in the lines. In fact, they ignore them! There is a sense and wonder in a child that screams possibility!

> **When I'm not feeling creative, I just turn off the computer, sit back, take a sip of coffee, and say to myself, "Hey, I can ALWAYS get another job, such as a coal miner." And then I turn the old computer right back on and become AMAZINGLY creative.**
>
> **Dave Barry**

Science confirms that children think with the front part of their brain, which is why childhood is the most creative time in a person's life. Over time, adults learn to be more cautious about processing information, which slows down the creative process. It takes self-discipline for an adult to be kid-minded.

Kids are curious. Curiosity is the first step to ingenuity. Kids ask a ton of questions. They don't settle for an easy answer, even if an adult has just told them "because I said so." Kids can put wild combinations together and not think twice about them. They see things differently than we do.

One day when Raegan was about four years old, I was pulling weeds out of my garden when I heard her excitedly yell, "Daddy, come over here." I rushed over only to see her bent down pointing at a bright yellow dandelion. I said, "I know, that's not good, is it?" She looked up at me with a puzzled look, pointed back at the dandelion, and said, "No, look!" After a few moments it hit me. I said, "Ohhhh, a flower!" She jumped up and down and said, "Yeahhh! A flower!" It is all in your perspective. I was looking with the wrong set of lenses.

Kids have fun. If you asked Raegan what she does for a living, she would say, "Play." Ask her what her favorite school subject is and she will tell you, "Recess." Kids take fun very seriously. When was the last time you had serious fun? Does life really have to feel like a three-piece suit and taste like medicine? Can ministry in the church be fun and not stressful?

We must never take ourselves too seriously. Time is too short and seriousness doesn't get us anywhere anyway. It is time to fire up the playful part of the brain again and watch the creative self emerge.

Jesus said, "My yoke is easy and my burden is light" (Matthew 11:30). Lord, please help us become like little children!

2. Creation-minded

A good acquaintance of mine, Mark Scandrette from San Francisco, held an event called UNTITLED 9.30.01. It was described as an "incubator for integrating life in the kingdom of God with the personhood and craft of the artist in the context of culture." Mark wrote some guiding perspectives for the event:

> We believe that we were created in the image of God and fulfill our identity and purpose partially through engagement in the creative process. We were made to discover and create.

Are you a creation? Created in the image of God? Do you believe the created reflects the image and characteristics of the Creator? Inside you is the most creative force in the universe, the Spirit of the living God. This should mean that Christians in church ministry and in the marketplace can and should produce the most creative ideas! Too often, though, it seems that capitalism triumphs over kingdom (at least on earth).

> **The imagination is among the chief glories of being human. When it is healthy and energetic, it ushers us into adoration and wonder, into the mysteries of God. When it is neurotic and sluggish, it turns people, millions of them, into parasites, copycats, and couch potatoes.**
>
> **Eugene Peterson, *Under the Predictable Planet***

The problem starts with the fact that our education system has pushed creativity right out of most of us. Neil Postman said it best, "Children enter school as question marks and leave as periods." We need to heed the advice of Mark Twain, "Never let formal education get in the way of your learning." It is never too late to rekindle creativity. It is still there inside you and in greater quantities than you realize.

More problems arise when we listen to the voices that tell us we are not creative. Do not give in to the false idea that you are not creative. In John 10:10, Jesus tells us: "The thief comes only to steal and kill and destroy; I have come that they may have life, and have it to the full." Fatalistic thoughts are a death-trap to creativity. This type of thinking plays right into the Devil's playbook: "Stay between the lines." "Don't pick up that musical instrument." "Do you really think you should be painting?" "You, creative? Ha!" These aren't God thoughts at all! You can try something new. You can step out of the box. You can walk on water if God wants you to.

3. You-minded

This one sounds a little self-serving. But what I am trying to say it that it's okay to be different, even weird. The postmodern world not only knows this, but delights in this fact. Here is an area where Christians should be making a mark. The Bible revels in diversity from the wild creation accounts in Genesis, to Jesus' revolutionary tendencies, to Paul's discussion of the parts of the body and spiritual gifts in Romans and 1 Corinthians. Yet, it seems that we Christians can be some of the most conforming people around. Yes, we want to conform to the image of Jesus Christ, but that does not mean that the Lord wants us all to look and act the same! You are who God made *you* to be.

At a recent national talent competition in a particular Christian denomination, a judge docked five points from a young woman's performance because she was wearing sandals. Never mind that her song blew away the audience and the other two judges. Somehow wearing a certain item of clothing was seen as less spiritual and therefore made the piece an "inferior" work.

What are some other examples of Christian conformity that you can think of? How about our music styles sounding alike? How about the look of our sanctuaries? What about our worship service schedules?

> **Leave the beaten track occasionally and dive into the woods. Every time you do so, you will be certain to find something that you have never seen before. Follow it up, explore all around it, and before you know it, you will have something worth thinking about to occupy your mind. All really big discoveries are the result of thought.**
>
> **Alexander Graham Bell**

Are we becoming franchises?

Fast Company, a business magazine geared for leaders on the edge, features a column with travel tips by sales people and executives who are away from home regularly. In the September 2000 issue, the columnist said, "When I'm on the road, I always go to church, because no matter where you are, it's exactly the same." Ouch.

In the most humble spirit you can, be who you are and let others be who they are. Getting rid of conformity will help us shake off the need to be like the better-known church across town. This will allow a local, indigenous, creative expression of Christianity to emerge. One that allows you to reach your tribe using their language, not the language of www.somebodyelsesministry.com.

> **Even if you're on the right track, you'll get run over if you just sit there.**
>
> **Will Rogers**

4. No-fear-minded

When I first started in ministry, a coworker of mine said something that still rings in my ears. He said, "Out of all of the motivations in life, I believe that fear is the greatest motivator of all time." The Bible tells us there is only one healthy fear (of God). Any other kind of fear is unhealthy. Second Timothy

1:7 says that a spirit of fear does not come from God. The source is pretty unpleasant, if you think about it.

If we don't confess and forsake our fears, they keep us from being the persons God intended us to be. Becoming a dad has given me a whole new perspective on my relationship with God. When my daughters are at play or attempting something new for the first time, my heart rejoices. I delight in watching them have fun and go exploring. This is also true of our heavenly Father. He delights in watching you step out of the boat. Conversely, he is saddened when you begin to sink by taking your eyes off of him.

Probably the biggest fear I have witnessed is the fear of rejection. This leads to a fear of failure and ultimately to a fear of trying. My hope is that the Church on the other side (to echo a phrase from pastor and author Brian McLaren) is one that actually embraces change and encourages innovation. That type of church will also have to be accustomed to failure. The last time I had an interview for a ministry position, the person interviewing me said: "At our church, we will attempt some things and we will fail. We like to laugh about our mistakes and learn from our failures." As soon as those words rolled off his tongue, I was ready to sign.

Imitation is suicide.

Ralph Waldo Emerson

The take-off

Now that you are feeling young again and your mind has been liberated from the sin of creative lethargy, it is time to take that creativity and channel it into idea creation.

I had a boss once tell me, "I do not get excited about good ideas, only good results." The problem with this blanket statement is that it squelches innovation. Real innovation, the kind we need in the Church, begins with the creation of ideas.

I see idea creation a little like an airplane ride. There is the take-off, air time, and landing of an idea. The take-off is about stimulus gathering. Air time is about making connections. The landing concludes the flight by grounding it in reality or putting the idea into practice.

In the take-off, we gather raw materials that will help spur thinking. It takes ideas to make ideas. In childlike fashion, it is important to become curious in *all facets* of life.

The original Renaissance man was Leonardo da Vinci. In one of his writings, he stated:

> I roamed the countryside searching for answers to things I did not understand. Why shells existed on the tops of mountains along with the imprints of coral and plants and seaweed usually found in the sea. Why the thunder lasts a longer time than that which causes it and why immediately on its creation the lightning becomes visible to the eye while thunder requires time to travel. How the various circles of water form around the spot which has been struck by a stone and why a bird sustains itself in the air. These questions and other strange phenomena engaged my thought throughout my life.

That was one curious mind. Asking questions about things you take for granted is a great way to open our eyes to new stimulus.

Another great way is to break out of routine. Why not drive a different route to work or school or home? If you have a job, get out of the office! (Especially if you are on staff at a church.) Whenever possible, spend more time outside the walls of your office than inside where the air can get a little stale.

In her book *The Artist's Way*, Julie Cameron offers a great suggestion for creative stimulus...the artist date. It is a date with yourself and the Holy Spirit (the last part is my addition). She defines it as "an excursion, a play date that you preplan and defend against all interlopers." Along the trip, pack all of your senses and use them. Go to a museum, a junkyard, a park, a coffeehouse, or a train station. Pray that God would inspire you to see things differently.

> **I want to thank anyone who spends part of their day creating. I don't care if it's a book, a film, a painting, a dance, or a piece of theater, a piece of music—anybody who spends part of their day sharing their experience with us.**
>
> **Filmmaker Steven Soderbergh**

Breaking out of your routine is especially important if you normally receive input from the same people over and over. This causes what I call "Group-Stink." You have been around the same people so long that your ideas usually fall down the same path. The Church can create some of the most offensive odors from this condition. It is like your family routines. No matter how old you are, when you go back home, you settle into your same old role. Instead, you need new sources of input.

One way to guard against this is to find creative people and surround yourself with them. I am somewhat of a controlled-creative type (if there is such a thing). Sometimes my creative perspective becomes too limiting. I have a group of people I hang out with whom I call my creative mojo. These artist friends help me see well beyond my standard spectrum of colors. They see ultraviolet colors that my eyes cannot find.

One of the friends in my mojo group is Ryan. Ryan has a new dream to tell me almost every week. These dreams are epics and never take less than an hour to tell. Personally, I am lucky if I remember a dream. His dreams have chapters! He is also one of the most creative people that I know. He keeps me fresh. When I am getting a little stale in the creativity department, I know it is time for some Ryan caffeine to give me a little creative stimulus.

Another routine buster is to do things you would not normally do. A friend of mine, Kevin Salkil, tells me that he finds much of his creative inspiration from tabloid magazines. We were in Seattle at a conference when he walked into our room with a copy of one of these popular tabloids under his arm. I asked him if I could look at it. He handed it to me and on the cover was batboy. It was a touching story of a young boy who had the unfortunate fate of being born with many bat-like features. He had the ears, the nose, and fangs of a bat. Bizarre? Yes. Sad? Yes. Creative? Definitely.

Another great place to get ideas is in the everyday repetitions of life, such as taking a shower, shaving, mowing the lawn, driving a car, doing the dishes. Einstein once said, "Why do I get all of my best ideas in the shower?" All of us have a logic side and a creative side—they are the right and left sides of our brain. When we do mundane everyday tasks, it keeps our left side (logic brain) busy. This frees the right side up to think up new ideas. So, keep a notepad in the bathroom and an audio recorder in the car.

Your sons and daughters will prophecy,
your young men will see visions,
your old men will dream dreams.
Even on my servants, both men and women,
I will pour out my Spirit in those days.

Acts 2:17–18

Air time

The next step is to take all of these great pieces of information and creative thoughts and actually do something
with them. This is where connections are made. You must
look at your stimulus from all sides—frontward, backward,
and upside down.

Sometimes it helps to also survey ideas from another
field. Buy a trade magazine for business, entertainment,
science, or education. Some of the greatest ideas of all
time came from people connecting ideas from places
nowhere near their field of endeavor.

This is where the "what-if" mode comes in. Asking
what-if questions allows the mind to daydream a little.
The idea for Experiential Storytelling started when I asked
the question, "What if we took all of the rules of a conventional retreat and did the opposite?" To begin, I listed all
of the elements of a conventional retreat on my white
board. Then one by one we asked "what if" questions.
*What if we had no speaker? What if we allowed the story to
speak for itself? What if the worship was not controlled but
participatory?* The answers to those questions became an
off-road adventure.

I have found this "what-if" mode is more enjoyable if done with other people. Grab a few creative types and ask for their opinions. Talking about an idea out loud is especially important if you are someone who needs to process verbally.

The landing

Now it is time to bring your sleek new airplane in for a landing. An idea is just that unless you ground it in some sort of reality. Creative thoughts must land on the runway of application.

If you have a team working with you on an idea, this is the time to ask the Holy Spirit to help you delegate properly. The key is surrounding yourself with good people and being bold in your implementation. Again, it is helpful being in a church structure that allows for innovation, but that is not always the case.

Even at NewSong, my first attempt at Experiential Storytelling was met with some silence from my boss. He had never seen something like this attempted and so naturally was a little skeptical. The design team knew that this was going to be a strikeout or a home run. The only way to evaluate the outcome, of course, was to put the ball into play and see what happened. We invited my boss along to participate (make sure you have the mind of God before doing this). He not only found the event to be powerful, but he wound up being a champion of this and other creative ideas. "Victories" like this will seed the ground for further innovation.

I'm writing this chapter passionately because there is so much at stake. I believe in the church. Christ died for it, and the Spirit moves it. Further, it is the primary instrument God has chosen to use on earth. If that is not a reason to be more creative in our communication, then I am at a loss. I hope that you can be a part of the creative conversation that is taking place in churches around the United States and the world. I also hope that you can be a part of creating a culture of creativity in your church that will eliminate the restraints on innovation. Let us use the Holy Spirit to help us break out of old molds and participate in transforming culture.

It is a daunting but not impossible task. Get on the creative plane and see where it takes ~~you~~ us.

CHAPTER FOUR

RE:IMAGINING
"THE SERMON"

"You cannot tell people what to do, you can only tell them parables; and that is what art really is, particular stories of particular people and experiences."

W.H. Auden

Here is an old logic problem that you have probably seen and tried many times. There are nine dots arranged like this:

·   ·   ·

·   ·   ·

·   ·   ·

Your task is to connect all nine dots by drawing four straight lines. You cannot retrace your lines or raise your pencil from the paper. Take a minute and try it. What you realize is that it is impossible to do the assignment without stretching outside the boundaries.

Nobody except the preacher comes to church desperately anxious to discover what happened to the Jebusites.

Harry Emerson Fosdick

In this chapter, I am going to ask you to do the same thing with your assumptions about what a sermon is or is not. In other words, stretch your thinking beyond a three-point message with punchy illustrations or topical exposition. Go beyond a homily that leads the listener to the speaker's desired outcome. Push your imagination to a place that goes beyond traditional boundaries, to a place where the story is the message and the message is the story. This will take considerable effort. Why? Because underlying assumptions often can be subtle and extreme-ly powerful.

So, if you feel a little uncomfortable, you are not alone. For centuries, we have been subtly conditioned concerning the form, the texture, and even the outcomes of a sermon.

> **We need to be specialists in imagery, pictures, symbols, and joyful metaphor. Our speaking needs not only to be explanatory but evocatory. We need to practice the hypothesizing, projecting, and anticipating that will allow artistry to communicate passionate urgency.**
>
> **David Larsen, *Telling the Old, Old Story***

For many, what comes to mind about sermons is sitting in a church building in an uncomfortable chair and listening to a man speak for a half hour to an hour while planning the rest of the week in their head, on a church handout, or on a PDA. These stereotypes have made their way into everyday vernacular: "Stop preaching at me." "Papa don't preach."

In today's more conservation-minded climate, preaching comes across as a tool from the era of conquest. Being preached at is like a one-sided battle in the age of the Crusades.

While the sermon has taken its much-needed lumps, there are some encouraging signs for the sermon. In recent years, the sermon has undergone serious scrutiny that has caused many to rethink its purpose and delivery. Much of this dialogue centers on a shift from propositional preaching to narrative preaching or storytelling. Still, propositional preaching is the most common form of preaching today.

"Blah, blah, blah..."

what the average person hears during a sermon

The goal of propositional preaching is to give a set of proofs (usually given the name "points") to bring the listener to a logical conclusion. The desire is to change the listener's mind on a topic by presenting facts to support the claim.

In contrast, narrative preaching is a method of speaking in story that is more intuitive and democratic in its approach. The focus is less on proving a point than telling a story. The story can speak on more than one level and be less threatening to the listener. Each message might affect a group of listeners in several different ways, each way relevant to a particular subset of listeners.

Preach the gospel at all times. If necessary, use words.

St. Francis of Assisi

This shift from propositional to narrative preaching will be a challenge to those who believe our current preaching style was handed down from God himself. The reality is that propositional preaching was developed a few centuries ago to accommodate cultural and technological transitions at that time. Lecture style preaching made sense in an increasingly modern society. It presented facts to the "class" seated in the "classroom." What was cutting edge ages ago, however, is making less sense all the time.

The shift to narrative is another adaptation to an increasingly postmodern cultural climate. In his book *Thinking in Story*, Richard Jensen says:

> We have been preaching three-point, linear, logical, analytical sermons for a long time! What we have often failed to do, however, is to understand that this form of preaching was given its shape by the form of the human communication of writing and print. As we move from a literate to a post-literate era we must become cognizant of the impact of media on our preaching and ask how preaching in our time might be shaped by our electronic forms of communication.

By *post-literate*, Jensen is not saying that we are moving toward an illiterate society. What he is saying is that we are moving away from the literacy of word to other forms of literacy. As Tony Schwarz says, "Electronic media rather than the printed word are now our major means of non-face-to-face communication." This is not the first major cultural shift in communication and—in this day of fast-moving technological advances—it will not be the last.

The matrix

A few years ago I came across something that helped me better understand these communication and societal changes. Rex Miller unveiled in a Leadership Network publication what he calls the Millennial Matrix. His grid is helpful because much of the recent discussions on the "new church" have centered on the philosophical shift from modernism to postmodernism. Rex's model incorporates this shift, but also focuses on significant communication shifts throughout the ages. A few years ago, he spoke to the magnitude of today's communication change by stating, "When the dominant means of storing and distributing information changes, so does the world in which we live."

> ## Church can be fun. Preachers can bring it alive with music, dancing, and Tai Bo.
>
> ## Bart Simpson

In his matrix, Rex charts the communication changes from each era that were introduced by technological advances. From 4000 B.C. until the 1500s, the primary communication mode was in an oral/aural form. The telling of stories was the primary method of learning and sharing history. The early church tradition was liturgical. Rituals, symbols, and storytelling were employed in worship and in the relating of the gospel.

From the 1500s until the mid 20th century, the primary communication mode was in the form of the printed word. Johann Gutenberg's invention of the printing press changed the nature of learning and the nature of communicating. Literature soon was in the hands of the masses, which accelerated the age of Enlightenment. The church tradition birthed out of this period came from Martin Luther's reformation movement. Communicating the Christian faith moved from storytelling to logical arguments and answers.

The 20th century brought about the most rapid changes in technology and communication ever witnessed in human history. The invention and cultural acceptance of radio and television marked a move into the broadcast age. Many churches adapted to this style in their services by making them more celebratory in nature. Programs and performance made the platform a stage of sorts with the congregants mere spectators. It was out of this time that much of the challenge to develop narrative preaching began to spring forth.

Then in the latter part of the 20th century and early 21st century, another even larger communication change occurred. That change is the transition from broadcast to digital—or to what Rex calls interactive—modes of communication. The Internet, MP3s, DVDs, PDAs, cell phones, and other newer digital technologies have contributed to this interactive explosion. It is impossible to think that these technologies, which have become fully integrated parts of our lives, will have little or no impact in our churches. According to Rex, this new communication mode is moving the church into a time of inclusion and participation with the audience. Worship becomes collaboration, faith now becomes a journey, and the gospel is now communicated in multiple forms and media.

This digital revolution has already transformed the communication landscape. The sermon has been undergoing transformation for years. The first wave of preaching "reforms" came from those extolling the benefits of narrative preaching. This form will continue to be influential in a deconstructed world where intellectual "enlightenment" has yielded once again to mystery.

In today's increasingly participatory climate, the message itself is moving toward the interactive. Adding to the recipe of exposition and narrative preaching, then, comes the collaborative experience. This moves us outside the grid of nine dots we looked at above. The dots are not erased, but the lines of possibility extend beyond the borders of current reality.

The stakes are high. In his book *Visual Faith*, William Dyrness states:

...our children and their friends have been raised in a different world; they are looking for a new imaginative vision of life and reality, one they can see and feel, as well as understand. And their attention spans for sermons and lectures are notoriously short! We, of course, believe that the Bible and the Christian tradition are primary resources for a recovery of vision. But we must listen carefully to this generation and reread Scripture in the light of their dreams and fears. Then perhaps we will present the gospel and plan our worship in ways that respond to their quest and reintegrate words and image. It is possible that we might actually win the battle of words but lose the battle of images. And losing that battle could well cost us this generation.

What if we attempted to move the preacher from a sermon-giver to a narrator telling a story? And what if the narrator is also a *guide* along the path of experience? We will explore what this looks like in greater detail in the next two chapters.

The story is no longer simply heard, but also experienced. With this experiential immersion, the "hearer" can listen on several levels and receive what's communicated in a form that disarms any fears of conquest. Experience by nature has a collaborative feel. It engages more of our senses and gets individuals involved in the story.

Storydwelling

Modernity has placed a lab coat on most preachers. After peering at the Bible under the microscope, they continually find more evidence and facts to disseminate to a waiting audience. The pressure each preacher faces is to come up with more and more points to explain what the text means.

> The church should tell the truth in all genres [and] relate the message of the gospel as comedy, tragedy, and fairy tale. Hollywood consistently beats the church at its own game.
>
> **Frederick Buechner**

Why not take a breather for a time and let the story speak for itself in a language those gathered can understand? When presented without all of the trappings of exegetical interpretation, the biblical text is freed from the limits of our minds and is open to the organic beauty of the infinite Word.

What will it take?

First, you and I must humbly acknowledge that we do not have all of the answers. And that is okay. I do not believe that God expects us to. God wants us to *stop trusting ourselves* and instead trust that the biblical text, as translated into contemporary English, can speak for itself.

> **[W]e were conditioned to speak of "building the sermon" through outlines, points, and theme sentences. But if, however, human experience is inherently temporal, a homily will be designed to shape experience rather than assemble thoughts.**
>
> **Richard Esslinger**

The next step is to pray and ask God to help us to *trust those attending our gatherings*. Trust that they can understand Scripture more clearly and better retain what they have learned when they're allowed to think for themselves.

The final step is to *trust the Holy Spirit*. He knows your audience far better than you do. He is the one who calls them to himself. He can give them the necessary interpretation.

Isn't this what we see in Scripture? Jesus used his surrounding environment to speak in stories and later, if necessary, to explain the deeper meanings of some of those stories. Before his death, Jesus went on to promise that the Holy Spirit would be our counselor and interpreter.

Now, here we are, Jesus Christ's body, whom he has entrusted to tell his story! Every now and then, let's step out in faith beyond the boundaries of traditional sermon preaching, try new forms of communication, and trust God for the results.

CHAPTER FIVE

ELEMENTS OF
EXPERIENTIAL
STORYTELLING

"Eugene O'Neill, the first great American playwright [1888-1953],
spoke freely of his hopes and dreams for a new kind of American
theater, one in which the audience might participate more vitally
and fully. He hoped someday to write plays in which the audience
could share as a congregation shares in the music and ritual of a
church service. 'There must be some way that this can be brought
about,' wrote O'Neill. 'As it is now, there is a too cold and cut
division between the stage and the auditorium. The whole
environment—stage and the auditorium, actors and spectators—
should be emotionally charged. This can only happen when the
audience actively participates in what is being said, seen, and
done. But how? That is the problem. Still, there must be a way.'"

Eric Miller in a paper on African folklore

The Journey Begins

In many ways it was a typical Tuesday morning in Cleveland—mostly cloudy and cold. On Tuesdays I held a weekly meeting in my corner office with my intern, Mike Gustafson. This morning my wife would be joining us. On my way to work, I turned the radio down, altered my path by taking a different road into the office, and began to pray. What started out as an ordinary day set me on a journey that has been anything but typical.

The wake-up call I described at the beginning of chapter 1 had led me to seriously critique the effectiveness of our church's youth ministry. Critique is not something I enjoy in ministry. It requires self-analysis and, more painful, other people's perspectives. To me, good critique is like medicine. Initially, I get a bad taste in my mouth and my internal defensives kick into high gear. But eventually I begin to feel better as the medicine does its work.

The key, then, is to ask people you trust to give you their critique and then deal with any defensiveness on your knees in prayer before meeting with them. I had both of these things going for me that morning.

Specifically, I was concerned about how well the teens in our church understood the story of Jesus Christ. Further, was it just a story to them? Was the story making any difference in their lives or was it just another fairy tale?

Some of our teens could recite the story of Jesus like the Pledge of Allegiance. Others didn't have a clue about the story, but liked hanging out with their friends.

> **We have now become aware of the possibility of arranging the entire human environment as a work of art, as a teaching machine designed to maximize perception and to make everyday learning a process of discovery.**
>
> **Marshall McLuhan**

Armed with a Bible and a blank white board, we prayed that the Holy Spirit would give us creativity to communicate the story in a language that our church's teens would understand. It was a sincere and desperate prayer from youth leaders seeking a better way.

We had done our homework by studying our young people and the dominant postmodern culture in which they lived. We observed that we had media-savvy teens who responded to symbols, imagery, and personal participation. These modes of communication were sorely lacking in any of our previous ministry efforts. Worse, we realized the Bible was full of amazing surround-sound imagery that we had turned a deaf ear toward while using a standard lecture-like teaching style that came across with all the fullness of AM radio.

Tell me and I forget, teach me and I may remember, involve me and I learn.

Benjamin Franklin

We had also witnessed firsthand a generation that was unafraid to ask questions and was tired of being told what to believe. They needed to be challenged, but not in the style we had been employing. They wanted to be moved, but were not going to budge by a story that had lost its richness and therefore most of its meaning. What was birthed from that morning was a template for a weekend retreat that eventually became known as the Jesus Journey. It also formed the backbone of what I now call Experiential Storytelling.

In the next chapter I'll present greater detail about the specifics of the *Jesus Journey*. Right now I want to give some thoughts on creating an Experiential Storytelling event. Remember this is an experimental genre—one that I hope will evolve. While writing this book, my prayer has been that whoever reads this book and applies it will also add to it. One way to do that is to log on to www.experientialstorytelling.com and share how you've created your own fourth-dimensional story.

Most of the principles I discuss below can be used in a one-hour service, but in this context I'll be describing a longer event. If you're not a gifted planner, be sure to include an event planner on your creative team.

Storyweaving

Think of your event as a blank canvas. Your palette is story and your paintbrush is experience. Take the theme of your story and ask yourself, *How can I use experience to paint a picture of this idea? How can I tell the story in a way that participants will feel it?* Ultimately, you need to ask how you can allow space for participants to paint their own stories onto the canvas.

The story is the point. The point is the story. The event is merely an excuse to tell that story. Every aspect of this event needs to be touched by the story. You must look at every angle of your event and look for ways to weave the story into every part.

Start with your advertisement. How can this be an introduction to your story? Do you want to foreshadow what is to come or provide some clues to whet their appetite? Prior to your event, think of ways you could build anticipation by dropping other hints. The Internet makes it easy to do this through updated Web pages and e-mail. Why not create a fictitious blog that would be a journal of someone in your story? By starting the story prior to the event, you can set the mood and tone.

Caution: Don't give away too much. If you begin to get too specific, you may end up tampering with the intrigue and integrity of your experiential story.

Then you take your story and weave it into your location. Be intentional about everything! Starting with their entrance into the parking lot, think about ways you could incorporate story into each participant's experience. Think through: Where do you want them to park? What door do you want them to enter? What does the door look like? Should there be someone greeting them at the door? What hallway should they come down? What does the hallway look like? Should they enter the room right away or should they wait? If they wait, what will they be doing there? And after considering each of these questions, add one more, "Why?" That will help you be intentional about every detail.

If you wanted to tell the story of creation in your event, how would you tell it? Would you progressively tell the story beginning in the parking lot or wait until participants enter the room? How would you weave "let there be light," "God created the heavens and the earth," "plants and animals," "Adam" and "Eve" into your event? What would be some mediums you could use? Why would you use one medium over another? Would you use art? How? Could the audience participate in the creation? Dream...

The fun of using this genre of communicating is exploring all of the creative possibilities. Everything is now fair game to help tell the story. The only limit is your imagination. Your use of varied media will help to reinforce the story's message and allow it to speak to participants on multiple levels.

This is what makes this approach so attractive. As part of his unique creation, God has wired each of us differently. Each person is a unique piece in the mosaic of his kingdom. Some individuals respond well to audio stimulation while others respond more to visual stimulus. Still others may find role-playing the key to bringing a story alive. Whatever the case, using different media will help to personalize your story in a way that simply telling it cannot.

So do not limit yourself as to what can and cannot be part of the story. Your invitation to the event can be part of the story. If the group needs to drive somewhere, your transportation to a new location can be part of the story. Your room (or lack of one) can be part of the story. The participants can go from spectators to active collaborators in the story. Even *you* can jump in and out of the story. By leaving open all possibilities, you allow experience to become the storyteller.

> **A soul never thinks without a picture.**
>
> **Aristotle**

Now let's look at some of the elements that might become a part of your experiential story.

Setting and Senses

Physical space

The moon is full, the crickets are chirping, the fire is roaring, and the marshmallows are dripping off the end of your stick. Where are we? At a camp-out. And what happens next is no surprise. It's time for someone to spin a ghost story. Told during the day or in a house, these stories would do nothing more than bore the hearer. Told out in the wild and especially at night, the heart beats faster, the goose bumps multiply, and the average storyteller becomes Stephen King. Simply put, setting matters.

In Experiential Storytelling, the setting is one of the main "characters" in your story. In a story, the setting is where the scene is taking place. It is the place where the character, conflict, and plot are introduced. In Experiential Storytelling, the setting does not mean that you recreate a particular type of setting. Instead, the setting in Experiential Storytelling is more about creating a space that speaks to the idea or message you are trying to convey. It is adding three-dimensional texture to the story. And since it is probably your participant's first impression of the story, it should immediately set the mood and tone.

Ideally, the site itself would be part of the story by nature of its setting. A synagogue, a theatre, the woods, a campsite, a stadium, and a basement are some potential sites for stories that come with built-in expectations. But it's not a problem if moving offsite isn't an option. Simply choose the best space you have available. Using that space to tell your story will greatly enhance each person's experience.

During our family's trip to Disneyland, we decided to go on the Indiana Jones ride. What continues to stand out in my mind was that the wait in line was almost as much fun as the ride itself. This was a good thing because the ride was only five minutes long, but the wait in line took an hour! The atmosphere created during that hour in line turned a mediocre ride into a real experience. A lot happened during those sixty minutes. We walked through a thick jungle complete with animal sounds and a cool mist hanging in the air. We then moved into a cavelike tunnel littered with lassos, faux fire, and bones. We weren't on a ride—we were on an excavation! Along the way, clues were given that pointed to the idea that something had gone wrong and that somehow our participation on this ride was going to be a part of the solution.

The good news is that you do not need a Disney-size budget or imagination to create the same type of feeling. Creating a setting can be as easy as turning the lights off or draining the room of noise.

For example, if your story is speaking to the issue of loneliness, think of ways you might use your space to speak to that. One way could be to place the participants in a dark setting. Lighting can create powerful settings. Silence could also be used to speak to this loneliness. Or you could combine the two elements to create a sense of outer space-like isolation. Another possibility is to go the opposite direction. You could use an overabundance of noise to create this same sense. Sometimes we feel the loneliest when there is too much noise around us.

> **We live in an age of the polymorphic massages of our senses.**
>
> **Richard Jensen**

Material world

Simple materials can be used to create a variety of effects. A friend of mine knew someone who owned a company that manufactured a metallic product. The waste byproduct created large rolls of what looked like aluminum foil. Since my friend had many rolls of this stuff, he asked if I wanted some. I loaded several into my car and on my drive home began to dream up multiple uses for these king-size rolls of faux Reynolds Wrap®.

In one of our experiential stories, we wanted to express a feeling of transcendence. With a room that had a nine-foot ceiling and brown carpeting, this seemed to be an impossible task. Enter the recycled Monster Wrap. We took pieces of this stuff and hung them from the ceiling. With some soft lighting reflecting on them, it created a very cool otherworldly effect. Since that time, whenever we want to create a transcendent or supernatural feel, we use this material. By darkening the rest of the room and putting a small lamp directly onto the metal, the room takes on a completely different feel. And by using the same material for different stories, it has become a familiar "character."

Caution: Don't put too many materials or props into a story. With every element discussed in this chapter you must ask yourself, How will this enhance or detract from the story? *You might find that a simple uncluttered room works best for your story.*

Here are some questions that might help you come up with ideas for settings. What setting would you use to communicate the idea of transcendence? How could you transform a room from a boring cube to an open-ended cathedral with a limitless sky? In what way could your participants begin to feel the mystery and wonder of creation? Or what about the power of the Flood or the subsequent wait for dry land? Or how would you create the feeling of freedom found in the Exodus story? For a stretching experience, imagine: How would you represent John's visions in the book of Revelation?

Coming to our senses

Studies have shown that only about 10 to 15 percent of what we "hear" comes in the form of spoken words. God has designed us to experience the world around us in all of its fullness, so most of our learning is nonverbal. We learn best when we use each of our senses, not just our sense of hearing.

Audio-visual caffeine

Well-placed visuals can be very effective in helping tell your story. This is a huge advantage over traditional storytelling. Lighting, physical symbols, artwork, texts, and video images leave impressions on the soul.

Following one moving Good Friday service, we set up a scene on the way to the exit. We used a sheet, a backlight, and a man lying on a cot with a blanket over him to create a silhouette. This was an element of surprise that greeted everyone when they stepped out of the sanctuary following the service. As they continued down the hallway, the words "and on the third day" were repeated over and over in various shapes, colors, and sizes. This was not a main part of the service, but it became a compelling image that left them with a sense of expectation.

Sound can be a great way to paint a picture. Radio commercials are a terrific source for ideas. I have heard several companies use sound to contrast their full-service companies with companies offering fewer options. These companies usually start with a single instrument as an example of a basic service. With the addition of each service, you can hear additional instruments blending in until finally you hear about their full-service options with the entire orchestra playing in the background. The musical selections are notable concertos, but you usually can't tell which song it is when only the oboe is playing. By adding other instruments, the song's identity becomes obvious and sounds robust. The commercials make their point; without that company's products, you might not be reaching your full potential. Think of how you could apply this to faith. When does faith sound flat and incomplete?

When you read the Bible, do you read it with a sense of sanctified imagination? Can you imagine the sights and sounds that must have been part of each scene?

Touchy-feely

Putting something in people's hands stimulates brain waves. Twila Edwards was a college professor who first taught this to me. She was the only teacher under whom I studied who actually encouraged doodling. I always found her to be an engaging professor. Some of my finest doodles came from her class on Essential Christianity. She believed the mind had the capacity to do more than one thing at a time and that doodling helped to keep the brain active during a lecture. How I wished some of my long-winded professors had held that same belief!

Play Doh® seems to have this same effect. Put Play Doh in people's hands and suddenly they become Michelangelo. Touch seems to be best applied as a response to the story. We will look into this more later in the chapter.

The nose knows

The sense of smell is strong and has a lot of experiential potential. My grandmother's old house had a certain smell that I run across every now and then. I will be in a mall or a store, catch the aroma of that smell, and suddenly feel like I am five years old standing in the guest bedroom in a small house in Miami, Oklahoma.

> **Art is the region between heaven and earth that connects the two.**
>
> **Mark Driscoll**

When I was seven years old, our neighbors' house burned to the ground. I walked past the charred remnants repeatedly the next morning. I can still instantly remember the smell of the wet burnt wood to this day. Saturday pancakes, Sunday night LaRosa's™ Pizza, and Mom's spaghetti are other smells that come back readily to me. What smells do you remember from your childhood? Okay, besides the locker room? What was it about each smell? Why is that smell still with you?

Jesus' friend Martha knew all about smell. Because of it, she initially resisted the Lord's command that Lazarus's tomb be opened. What smells must have greeted people when they entered the temple? The rancid smell of burning hair? Or the appetizing aroma of a BBQ?

What other biblical smells come to mind?

Taste and see

Taste is one of our most influential senses. In Scripture, we see taste most often in the form of meals. The meal has been a place of relationship, sharing, and servanthood. Jesus' Last Supper with his disciples is one of the most powerful statements on servanthood ever made. Whether we call it communion, the Eucharist, or the Lord's Supper, the meal itself has been a profound connecting point for believers down through the centuries. By creating a context and wrapping a story into it, that simple Passover (Seder) meal imparted much deeper meaning to Jesus' words about giving his body and blood as an atonement for our sins.

The Lord's Supper also represents a powerful metaphor for the Church. Since the Church is a family, the meal speaks of our family table as believers. For many, drawing out this type of symbolism can begin a healing process for many individuals.

Symbols and subtlety

Why would God fill his Word with endless symbols and imagery? Why would he use water, wind, fire, cloud, *and* light as symbols to speak about the Holy Spirit? Why not just fire? Or water? Why confuse us with so many symbols? Could it be that God knows that we have finite minds and need to receive truth in more than one dimension? For an indescribable God to reveal himself, he has to use a variety of symbols. One symbol or method of communication would fall dreadfully short of the glory of his splendor and creativity.

In his book *Ancient-Future Faith*, Robert Webber states that our task in a postmodern world is

> to understand and apply symbolism of atmosphere such as the sense of awe and reverence, to recover the beauty of space and the symbolic actions of worship, and to restore the sounds of music and the sights of the arts. For in these symbolic ways God's presence and truth are mediated to us. In these symbolic

actions we take the known and lift it into the unknown so that it is returned to us as the mystery of the transcendent.

These powerful metaphors speak to the imagination and soul. God has empowered us to use every creative impulse that we possess, individually and collectively, to mine the pages of Scripture and bring those compelling images back to the playground of the mind.

In Experiential Storytelling, images can be literal ones that have an immediate impact or abstractions that foreshadow a coming event. After determining the theme you want to convey through a particular part of the story, think about what image you may want to use to symbolize or communicate that idea.

On the following page are some random images from Scripture that have both literal and symbolic meanings. What ideas do these images represent or could they represent? (Use a Bible dictionary or concordance to explore these ideas further.)

Darkness	Light	Tree
Snake	Dirt	Ashes
Fruit of a Tree	Roots of a Tree	Vine
Branches	Apple	Sword
Boat	Fish	Rain
Fountain	Ark	Dove
Oil	Water	Fire
Smoke	Tower	Fortress
Garden	Door	Eye of a Needle
Currency	Sandals	Word
Bowl	Cup	Cross
Body	Robe	Curtain
Torn Curtain	Candlesticks	Jars of Clay
Salt	Aliens	Slaves
Master	Coin	Lion
Lamb	River	Stars
Trumpets	Beast	Dragon
Seed	Wheat	Horse
Bull	Scroll	Crown
Thorns	Wind	Bride
Throne		

Now think of how many ways you could incorporate one of these images into your story. Do not underestimate the importance of the symbol. In some instances, the symbol itself might become the main part of the story.

While reading the Gospel of John a few years ago, I was struck by his repeated use of images. He speaks about "light" 24 times, including three times in this short passage:

> Then Jesus told them [the crowd], "You are going to have the light just a little while longer. Walk while you have the light, before darkness overtakes you. The man who walks in the dark does not know where he is going. Put your trust in the light while you have it…" (John 12:35-36a).

Illustrations could do some justice to this passage, but what would happen if you could feel the darkness as these verses are read? Or what if you created a situation where the group walks through a lighted obstacle course and then walks the same course with the lights turned off? What if the narration is read when the group walks through with the lights off?

On one occasion I began to think about how empty darkness is and how a tiny ray of light could defeat it. The latter thought helped my team and me create a story of the ever-present struggle between light and darkness for one segment of the *Jesus Journey* discussed in chapter 6.

Even something as simple as using color can have representational meaning. What comes to mind when you think of the color red, blue, green, or gold? Now put these colors together with one of the images in the list above. What is the difference between a white robe and a scarlet robe?

By placing these images into your setting, using them in your story, or having them become the story, you speak to a deeper, more personal level. You also bring the images in the text to life in a way that simply reading or speaking them cannot.

Thou shalt be subtle!

Remember to let your audience think for themselves. Do not make everything obvious by spelling out every detail for them. This is where you are going to have to trust that your audience members have imaginative abilities and a built-in mechanism that allows them to think for themselves. It is called a brain. Too often we try to explain everything ad nauseam.

The key to a good experiential story is allowing subtle, seamless clues to reinforce the main idea or theme of your story. Through subtlety, participants are allowed to find personal meaning in the story. When we give them the answers, we violate the process by taking the thinking, imagination, and creative control from others. This often shuts them off because it violates trust. It also takes away from the mystery and surprise that a story and experience can provide.

> **Revelation in one sense is better sung or danced than read and outlined, for it is only in such dramatic images that the powerful presence of the Triune God, who gathers up all history into the final settlement, is properly experienced.**
>
> **William Dyrness**

The interplay between the surroundings, symbols, and participants is sacred. Presenting a story in such a way that participants can interpret the subtext for themselves is inherently interesting.

Participants will also appreciate that you are not preaching to them. As I've said before, there is a time and a place for traditional preaching. This is *not* that time. In fact, it is crucial that you do not start interpreting the experience for them. The whole point is the experience does the talking. Resist the urge to state its meaning.

Instead, let the Bible and the Holy Spirit speak for themselves. They are big enough to handle the job without our help! So trust the process. Trust your participants. And most importantly, trust the Holy Spirit.

Role-playing

Participants in Experiential Storytelling may be active or passive. The active participant plays a role that has direct input into the story. It is possible to assign roles to everyone if the experience requires it. In contrast, passive participants play a more indirect role in the story. These people are typically onlookers. Even if they don't add or detract from the story, they are still participants by virtue of stepping into the experience. You also may want to enlist one or more guides.

The active participant

The active participant is any player given a role in the story. These roles may include speaking or acting parts. Depending on the scene, they might also include direct interaction with passive participants. The important thing for these participants is not to come across as corny. They must appear natural with and blend into their given setting.

I have been to church productions that had centurion guards walking around in sandals, wearing leather skirts, with red peacock plumes protruding from their helmets. This is not natural! It might have been natural in A.D. 30, but it's hard to find anyone wearing centurion helmets and carrying Roman spears these days.

Remember, we are trying to bring an ancient story into today's language in every way possible. That does not mean, however, that you can never use symbols or props that have an ancient look to them.

Active participants should look so natural that many onlookers will not initially know who they are. One moment, a player might be sitting at a table casually conversing with several passive participants. The next moment, however, that person might step into the story by acting out a particular part. Take advantage of the element of surprise!

You can also surprise some of the passive participants by calling on them to become active participants. You can do this through improvisation or by giving each individual or team a defined role. With improvisation, you allow the participants to make up their own dialogue and "acting." This can be a lot of fun, but be prepared for a lot more variables in your story.

Either way, give newly recruited players a clear explanation of what to do and why they are to do it. Their task or role should not be too complicated and certainly not embarrassing. You never want to violate their trust.

The guide

Is it better to narrate or let the experiential elements speak for themselves? It's up to you and the right side of your brain. Use narration if words need to set the stage for the story. If not, the experience might be narrated with imagery and other sensorial textures.

The important thing is to provide guidance. Passive participants need enough information to allow them to have a proper expectation of why they are there and what they are to do. There are several ways to do this. One way is by giving them short, written instructions.

We put together an experience called "Stations Toward the Cross" that combined music, art, and props that gave a sobering, reverent look into the last week of the life of Jesus. Rather than narrate the event, we wrote out several passages of Scripture written on parchment paper in calligraphy. This written piece gave the necessary backdrop so people could prepare for and enter into the experience.

> **Postmodern theories of communication have shifted to the centrality of symbolic communication through an immersed participation in the event. This emphasis represents a shift from a print-oriented society to an audio-visual society.... [E]vangelicals will need to draw from the well of symbolic forms of communication.**
>
> **Robert Webber**

Another possibility is to ask someone to serve as the guide. The guide is an active participant. He or she enters the story as needed to provide instruction. When his or her instruction or narration is finished, the player steps back into the role of passive participant and enjoys the story with everyone else. The guide should never overshadow the story. Let the story speak for itself. The guide is certainly not the main character in the story. In fact, the guide is not even a character in the story. Rather, he or she provides just enough instruction to get the story going again. More than one person can serve as a guide during the course of a particular story.

In one scene of the *Jesus Journey*, I played the role of the guide. My job was to explain that a special guest wanted to share some thoughts with all of us. When we arrived as a group in what we called the journey room, we were met by one of our youth staff members, Zach, who began to recite the Sermon on the Mount word for word. (We had projected PowerPoint® slides on the back wall, but the group did not know this.) As soon as Zach was finished, he left the room. As a guide, I concluded the time by instructing the group about the next part of the story. The next time we saw Zach, he was no longer playing the Jesus role. He was Zach the youth staffer again—just another passive participant.

Choose your guides carefully. There is nothing worse than a guide who does not understand the story or the Experiential Storytelling process. (Make sure they read this chapter first!)

The passive participant

The passive participant is mostly an onlooker. Their main task is to experience the story. Think about where you want to place these passive participants, and how and if you want them to interact with other participants. Your choices will depend greatly on what you are trying to accomplish in the story.

Communal experience and personal expression

Once people have participated in an experiential story, it's helpful to ask for response or engage in a dialogue.

Response

The response time can be even more important than the story itself. The experiential story will most likely stir a lot of emotions in the hearts of participants. To finish the story and say "good night" would be a letdown.

Think of a time when you viewed a movie that stirred you deeply. What did you do? Did you spend a few moments by yourself as the credits rolled? Or did you go for coffee with a friend to talk about the movie?

Because the idea of Experiential Storytelling is to give participants a feeling of ownership, any response time should allow for a sense of personal connection. I believe the opportunity for responding to God always needs to be a personal one. We should give the participants an opportunity to respond, however, in the way God has wired them to respond. Some churches now use clay and other artistic tools to give individuals the freedom to uniquely express their response to God (and others).

Dialogue

While it is important not to provide all of the answers to participants, it is important to provide an outlet for discussion. A physical space and time allows them to share with others what they have just encountered. Their learning experience is enhanced when they hear the perspectives of others. Dialogue time helps verbal processors express themselves and provides nonverbal processors with an opportunity to think about what is said.

Most importantly, dialogue creates a sense of communal unity that comes from shared experience. The phrase "you would have had to have been there" often rings true. Many stories cannot be explained with mere words.

Your turn!

Now it's time to use your God-given creativity to come up with the basic sketch for an experiential story. This is probably an exercise better enjoyed by more than one person, so invite your creative mojo friend(s) to join you.

Use what I've written so far in this chapter to help you fill in the next few pages. You may want to review the list of symbols I gave you and try to incorporate some of them into your story. The next few pages are your canvas. There is no need to fill in every blank. One or two powerful thoughts might be enough to tell your story in an effective, experiential manner.

Begin by selecting one of the five well-known stories listed below. Then pray, asking God to help you turn that particular biblical narrative into an experiential story. Have fun!

Story Ideas

▸ **Creation**

▸ **The Exodus**

▸ **The Prodigal Son**

▸ **The Parable of the Seeds**

▸ **Good Friday**

Weaving the story

Will you present a single story or a series of stories? How will you create a physical space that helps tell the story? What is the mood of the story? How will this space help create that mood? Will you keep participants in one room or have them move to multiple spaces? Why or why not?

Engaging the senses

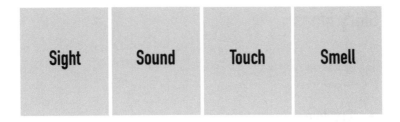

What setting will you use to tell the story? What materials will you use to create a variety of effects? Which of the five senses can you stimulate to add more texture to your story?

Symbols and subtle imagery

Remember, compelling images speak to the imagination and soul. God often uses multiple symbols to express or explain truths. Do the same! Use the list of random images on page 110 to help you come up with ideas.

Role-playing

Will you use a narrator? Why or why not? Will you use a guide to introduce your story or keep it moving? Why or why not? Will those attending be active or passive participants? Why or why not? How can you use role-playing to create a more intimate and participatory experience for the audience?

Communal experience and personal expression

How will you give people the opportunity to respond to or dialogue about the story? Will you allow for creative personal expression? Will you provide participants with a worship experience? Why or why not?

CHAPTER SIX

KILLER APPS

The combination of experience and participatory storytelling is not new. African storytelling is highly participatory and has been handed down for countless generations.
Improvisational theatre has incorporated the audience for
centuries.

What's new is how widespread this cultural shift
toward experience and storytelling has become. From
sports fantasy camps to contemporary art installations,
Americans seem to be craving greater interaction with all
parts of their world.

Let me give you several examples of how sensory experience and story are being used in popular culture and the Church. Perhaps these examples will be kindling for your own creative bonfire.

Theatre

In the first chapter I mentioned the popular comedy *Tony and Tina's Wedding*. The advertisement for the show reads "Tony and Tina are getting married and you're all invited." The rest of the evening is, well, a wedding! The evening has food, song, dance, and the rich family dynamics of an Italian social event.

Following the ceremony, the evening becomes an entirely interactive affair. You have no idea if the people at the table or on the dance floor are part of the audience or part of the cast. Many members in the cast add to the drama as they argue across the table and begin to include the audience in the fun.

Another example of successful experiential theatre is the musical *Mamma Mia!* The show uses the group ABBA's greatest hits woven into three love stories. Because of the audience's familiarity with the music, their participation becomes the main attraction.

Shows like Blue Man Group will feed your creative soul. Blue Man is a postmodern mime where blue alien-like men are the main characters of the show. They cannot speak and yet the message they communicate is heard loud and clear. At one of their shows my wife and I attended, Stacey leaned over to me at one moving part of the show and said, "This would be a great time for an altar call."

Feel the burn

Burning Man is an experience in radical expression. In 1986, two men decided to burn a man in effigy on a small beach in San Francisco. From this simple beginning came a weeklong event in the Black Rock Desert where 25,000 people pay $300 for a campsite to spend a week experimenting in art and community. They build their own dwelling structures, some several stories high, with all of the "streets" laid out in a perfect circle from the center of the city. The center happens to be the forty-foot high Burning Man. Participants create artistic pieces and design costumes that will be destroyed at the end of the week.

Every participant *experiences* art as he or she contributes creative offerings to the community. The freedom of structure and the ability to scratch the itch to create is a powerful combination that keeps people coming back. This phenomenon continues to attract more "burners" seeking meaning in experience.

There is a light that shines in the darkness....
His name is Jesus, the light of the world.

Deliriou5?

Each Burning Man week reflects a theme and each group or individual is encouraged to contribute their part to that story. Burning Man 2003 had a distinctly spiritual overtone. Titled "Beyond Belief," the Web site stated: "Beyond the dogmas, creeds, and metaphysical ideas of religion, there exists immediate experience. It is from this primal world that living faith arises." That says it all.

Sound installations

In a sound installation, the artist uses sound instead of paints or materials to create unique artistic sensory experiences. The installation is usually in a single room and sometimes will encourage participation from the viewer. Many of the installations combine mixed media elements to enhance the sound immersion experience.

Your local contemporary art museum probably would be a good place to find a sound installation. You might find them at your local colleges as well, particularly any art school. Many of these museums and schools are seedbeds for creative fruit.

Visual installations can also be creative candy, but often are less creative in their subtleties than the sound installations. I would encourage experiencing both.

The labyrinth

Probably the most widely recognized Christian experiential event is the labyrinth. Although the labyrinth has been around for thousands of years, many people are discovering its mystery and beauty for the first time.

If you are unfamiliar with a labyrinth, it consists of winding pathways that continue in one direction without a dead-end. The purpose is to create a symbolic path that gives each person space to contemplate the deeper issues of life while he or she quietly walks through the labyrinth.

One church in England has taken the traditional stationary labyrinth and created an experiential path.

Combining modern technologies such as compact disc players and video with more organic items such as water, rocks, and sand, this modern labyrinth is a journey for the senses. The experience was constructed to be a missional connect with postmodern culture. On their Web site (www.labyrinth.org.uk) they describe the purpose of their labyrinth:

> The language used and the whole labyrinth experience are full of imagination, artistic endeavor, images, symbols and metaphors that are evocative of the Holy, but retain some sense of mystery, that God cannot be fully explained. This type of language resonates with many of the spiritual seekers in our times who will willingly linger with the different dimensions to religious awareness afforded by things like candles, icons, silence, Gregorian chants and hints of mysticism.

The labyrinth differs from most Christian experiential stories because of its individualistic focus. I greatly enjoyed my own labyrinth walk, but my bias is toward communal learning experiences. Still, this idea is heading in the right direction.

A Seder

A Seder service is a great example of incorporating symbol, taste, touch, and smell into a story. I attended my first Seder service at NewSong when a friend of mine, Mona Stewart, began coordinating them.

The typical Jewish Seder tells the story of the Passover. A Messianic Seder adds a deeper dimension by relating how the life and sacrifice of Jesus fulfills the symbolism of many traditional Jewish Seder elements.

It would be no exaggeration to say that in recent centuries the printed word in theology has predominated over imagination, drama, myth, pictures, and storytelling. And yet few, if any, of our most fundamental Christian convictions can be reduced to words on a printed page. There remains in human beings a deep hunger for images, sound, pictures, music, and myth.

Bryan Stone, *Faith and Film*

The beauty of the service is how everything is done with intentionality. Wine serves as a symbol of joy and happiness. Salt water symbolizes tears. Bitter herbs symbolize suffering. Each taste allows the participant to more fully experience the Last Supper.

During a traditional Seder, questions are recited that allow both participation and anticipation. At one point children scramble to find a missing piece of matza—a mysterious symbol of the risen Messiah.

This ceremony is many centuries old, but it is experienced anew each spring.

Worshiptelling

A couple of years ago Tribal Generation sponsored an event called "Epicenter" at a church in Austin, Texas. My friend Andrew Jones related the event to me.

On one of the nights, they held a multilayered worship experience laced with symbolism. Participants had to enter the church through the small fire exit doors, instead of the large front doors, to symbolize the narrow way of faith. Four floors of experiential encounters were used to symbolize various aspects of the faith journey.

Several theme-based rooms on different floors represented various biblical images and stories. At one point, participants waded through trash, symbolizing sin. Later they put on white robes following an encounter with the cross.

The most profound part of the evening was the Eucharist service at the end. Everyone gathered in the sanctuary around a pile of garbage collected from the streets of Austin. The garbage again spoke of sin. The communion elements were taken from the garbage itself with the bread wrapped in an old cloth and the wine wrapped in a brown paper bag. Beauty and redemption sprang forth from the refuse meant for destruction.

This is a Web posting from someone who attended the gathering:

> To be honest, I've often forgotten the importance of the mysterious paradox at the heart of the Lord's Supper. God designed to come through the womb and become a man, and every time we partake of the communion cup and drink, we are partaking of his humanity and remembering that we've been gifted with resurrection in him. Many times I've gone up to take communion in my church after saying a simple prayer of repentance and thanks with little to no idea that I am again encountering Jesus the God-man, and the sacrifice he made for me. At this evening's service, in order to drink from the wine bottle and eat the bread, we had to wade through garbage. People were weeping around me. Some stood at the edges of the garbage, voluntarily wiping the communicants' feet as they headed toward the exit aisle. From the outside of the sanctuary, this may have looked like the most profane Eucharist ever. But as we broke Jesus' body with each other, I realized I had been profaning it for a long time.

Another church experimenting with immersive experiences in their worship is Westwinds Community Church in Jackson, Michigan. At an event called Velocity, they began the narrative of the evening the moment people stepped into the church. They expressed key themes in a variety of ways throughout the evening, seamlessly tying the evening together. During the large group portion of the evening, the church offered various stations where participants could personally respond to God.

> **The mind is insatiable for meaning, drawn from, or projected, into the world of appearances, for unearthing hidden analogies, which connect the unknown with the familiar, and show the familiar in an unexpected light.**
>
> **Arthur Koestler**

The Jesus Journey

My personal baptism in experiential learning came from a weekend getaway called the *Jesus Journey*. Originally called the *Jesus Freakend*, we envisioned the event as a way to connect our teenage audience to biblical stories through experience.

Our design team began with a blank white board and began putting the stories and experiential pieces into place. The brainstorming for the weekend dealt as much with what to cut as what to include.

For this first experimental step into this genre, we wanted an entire weekend to focus on the story of Jesus Christ. We knew we needed to start "in the beginning" where the need for a Savior began. So the journey begins in divine revelation and carries the REDemptive color of the blood of Jesus Christ throughout the weekend. Eventually, characters, images, experiences, narrations, personal stories, and large-group response all came together for an unforgettable weekend.

This retreat has come to be one of the most effective evangelistic events at the church. The most common comment we receive from retreat guests is that Jesus now seems real to them. Many young people hear about Jesus, but few get to know him. The *Jesus Journey* makes it personal. Since the first *Jesus Freakend*, many youth groups and postmodern ministries and churches have used this format with great results. I was surprised at how adaptable the elements were for a variety and diversity of groups.

Here is the blueprint for the weekend.

The *Jesus Journey* is laid out in a series of journeys that act like chapters in our story. Journey 1 begins in Genesis. The conclusion of the event is inspired from Acts, where the torch is passed on to participants.

Journey 1

This is the longest journey of the weekend and features the use of lights, sound, and narration. Our goal is to portray Creation through the coming of Jesus Christ.

Participants are led into a dark room and placed in one of many chairs. It is utter darkness. Eyes will not adjust to the light—there is none. Many people put their hands in front of their faces and sense nothing more than the current of air created by the movement. The darkness in the room is palpable and becomes one of the characters in the narrative without a single word being spoken.

Once everyone is seated, words pierce the darkness and give a brief introduction to the weekend. The voice explains that this room is a room of journeying together and that participants need to respect the experiences of those around them. The sense of mystery builds as the words fade into a poem that expresses the wonder of being involved in a supernatural journey.

Then the poem fades and the narrator's voice echoes as if he were in an empty room. He speaks of everyone being in an empty expanse, nothing above and nothing below. He describes how God decides to create and in one breath says, LET THERE BE LIGHT! At that exact moment thunder crashes and light fills the room. This light is not a natural light. It is man-made. But the light from that single bulb fills the room and causes most of the participants to cover their eyes.

The narrator talks about the other acts of creation and describes the harmony found in the garden. A symphonic melody plays in the background as descriptions of beauty and paradise unfold. Then the music begins to fade and the tone of the narrator changes as he tells of a presence—a dark presence—that also has access to this harmonious creation. The music begins to sound less harmonic and slightly eerie. Those seated cannot help but feel uncomfortable. This awkward sense continues until it crescendos with a simple sound—a bite of an apple. With that, the narrator explains that sin has entered the world and for the first time, the light begins to fade.

Over the next few minutes, the narrator tells of the hopelessness and despair of creation as sin continues to multiply out of control like a virus. He explains that God, in his infinite mercy, puts in place his plan to once again reconnect his creation to himself and restore the harmony that was damaged. He does this through a group of unlikely people. During this time the light seems to get brighter. But ultimately it fades as the narrator explains that humanity's attempts at restoration fail. A song of desperation and a plea for salvation now plays. By the end of the song, the light is nothing more than a dim, foglike presence in the room. It is a feeling of twilight. The feeling of hope lost leads to the uncomfortable sense that we are all about to plunge again into the dark abyss.

A piano is heard playing in the background. The song played is a slow and drawn out song. Over the top of this music, the narrator introduces the prophets—those handful of messengers through whom God speaks. Each voice explains that "salvation is coming!" One cries out to prepare the way of the Lord. Another speaks of the place where this Savior will come. And yet another speaks of a great light that is coming, a light so bright and terrible that everyone must cover their eyes. With each voice, the anticipation builds.

"And then," the narrator states—the voices fall silent.

Silence fills the room. A silence, the narrator explains, that becomes deafening to each person's ear. A silence that only a black hole knows. A black hole with no light and no sound. For four hundred years this silence continues. The people keep waiting, and waiting, and waiting and waiting. The narrator's voice fades and a faint heartbeat pulsates in the piano music. Eventually the music also fades until there is nothing.

No sound.

No light.

This lasts only a minute, but it feels like an eternity. The awkward pause here creates feelings of utter loneliness and isolation. The first darkness was tolerable because participants knew it would change. But this darkness is different because of the regression that has taken place since that first great (albeit man-made) light appeared.

After the pause hangs in the air, the silence and darkness are simultaneously overcome with the singing of the words, "There is a light that shines in the darkness." On the word "light," someone strikes a single match. The match immediately lights a single candle that is placed over a white cloth. The song goes on to say: "His name is

Jesus, His name is Jesus, light of the world." The music then fades into a subdued, ethereal, angelic-like song of praise. The narrator concludes by saying that darkness has now been defeated forever. This seemingly insignificant light has once again restored hope and salvation. A chorus of angels begins to sing out. Angelic harmonies now fill the room as the warmth of the candle shines its organic luminescence.

Following this first Journey, there is such an energy in the room. Participants have just heard and experienced creation and harmony, sin and isolation, and ultimately hope and joy. That energy needs to go somewhere.

> The new Mozarts may not be the ones simply composing music. They may be those people who create a dynamic compositional experience that enables people to comprehend how music is made, played, and understood. Excellence in interactive experience must be measured by the degree of conversation and transformation that occurs in the environment and the degree to which there is a shared sense that everyone is part of the process.
>
> **Edwin Schlossberg,** *Interactive Excellence*

As worship music plays in the background, the host instructs the group on the importance of responding to God in that moment. The audience is free to use their blank Jesus Journals, clay, paints, poetry poster, or story poster (for testimonies) to express what they have experienced. The creative inspiration unleashed during this response time is a thing of beauty.

Journey 2

The only teaching of the weekend takes place at this point when one of our weekend staff members temporarily portrays Jesus and recites the Sermon on the Mount. Participants are told to gather in what we call the Journey room. There they are told that an important guest has some things to share with them. The Jesus candle is still lit and now rests on a red blanket, foreshadowing his death.

The Sermon on the Mount is given by the Jesus figure (one of the staff for the weekend). He shares the entire sermon word for word. After he is through, he steps out and the weekend guide thanks the speaker and explains that our friend Matthew has promised to take notes on all that was spoken in case anyone missed it.

That is followed with a time for small group discussions about what the teens have experienced so far. These dialogue groups gather at strategic times throughout the weekend.

The first time I led this particular discussion, one of the participants looked at me and said, "That first journey was so dark, I couldn't even see my hands. I did not realize that is what we are like without God."

Another teen said, "That one-minute pause was the first time I have understood the intertestamental period. That was the longest minute of my life!" You can try to lecture on this waiting period until you are blue in the face. But when it is felt through experience, it finally hits home.

Journey 3

We desperately want teens to experience the ministry of Jesus Christ during the weekend. The first exercise during this third journey invites participants to interact with the meaning of Jesus' teachings. The second exercise gives them the closest experience to being healed that we can provide.

Parable stew

This is pretty simple. Every small group receives a list of the parables. Each group has to pick one of the parables and act it out. The teens can do this in any form of their choosing. Some have rapped their parable and others have acted them out. One group even tried to mime their parable.

The cup of afflictions

Just prior to Free Time, a guide announces with a deadpan face that a terrible disease has been making its way through the camp. He says that it affects people in different ways. A bowl is passed around and the guide tells the teens that whatever affliction was in that bowl has now struck them. Some teens are struck blind (using blindfolds), some lose the use of one arm or leg (using rope), and some are declared "unclean" (using signs). Those who are unclean cannot come with 15 feet of anyone (unless that other person is also unclean). They also must yell "unclean" wherever they go.

The guide explains there is no cure for this mysterious disease. They are told, however, that a rumor has been going around about man with a red blanket draped over his shoulder who has the power to heal.

It's interesting to watch the teens form communities based on their afflictions. The "lucky" ones with only an arm affliction occupy their time trying to find the man with the red blanket. This exercise goes on for about an hour. Finally, at long last, the Jesus figure steps onto the scene.

I recall the first time we did this. A teen is sitting on the floor with a blindfold over his head. He is rocking back and forth, very much into the part. The Jesus figure enters the room with the red blanket that had been under the candle during the second Journey. In perfect King James English, this Jesus person (who is unscripted) walks up to the blindfolded teen and says, "What troubles you, my son?"

The teen says, "I am blind, but I was told there was someone with a red blanket with the power to heal me."

The Jesus person replies, "Your faith has made you well." He takes off the teen's blindfold and sternly warns him, "Now do not tell anyone else about this."

Without hesitating, the teen runs upstairs shouting, "I'm healed, I'm healed!"

A swarm of young people suddenly rushes downstairs and through the back door after the man with the red blanket. Some teens lead their blind friends. Others carry the crippled.

Nothing prepared me for this next moment. The "mob" finally catches up with the Jesus person and gathers around him. One by one he touches them and removes whatever troubles them. As the signs, ropes, and blindfolds come off, the teens begin to jump up and down for joy. The Jesus person then walks into the midst of the "unclean" group and heals them.

The gospel has come to life for everyone involved.

Journey 4

The *Jesus Journey* storyline remains the same, but we try to add new components from year to year. After all, there are many ways to tell the same story. The Last Supper is a scene we have depicted in a variety of ways.

To highlight servanthood, those in leadership have served the tables and even taken the participants into separate rooms to wash their feet prior to dinner.

Another time the Jesus figure slipped back into his role and asked everyone to join him in drinking the cup and eating the bread. Judas was another youth staff member sitting at the same table as the Jesus figure. People were quite startled when he ran from the table, slammed the door, and ran out into the cold night—intent to betray his friend, their tablemate.

The element of surprise keeps participants guessing and adds to the feel of mystery. Even those who know the Jesus story do not know quite how it is going to be told.

Journey 5

After participants experience the light of Jesus, the healing power of Jesus, and the servant's heart of Jesus, Journey 5 is a jolting reminder of the sacrifice of Jesus Christ. The participants are again led into the Journey room. The only thing in the room is the Jesus candle on the red cloth.

A follower of Jesus acts as the narrator. He describes Jesus' arrest in the garden last night, expresses confusion over what is happening now, and reveals his deep fear that something terrible could take place at any moment.

At this point we show a short video clip depicting Jesus' journey to the cross and his crucifixion. When the words "It is finished" are spoken, the video is instantly unplugged and the candle goes out. The room is once again plunged into utter darkness. An extremely somber or confessional song begins to play.

After such a powerful emotional experience, we find that participants need the opportunity and time to respond. Sometimes we take communion and worship. Other times we allow teens to deal with the sin that has affected their lives.

Journey 6

Journey 6 takes place on the last morning. Everyone quietly makes his or her way to the Journey room. The same narrator in Journey 5 tells everyone he is upset that Jesus let him down. Like the rest of the disciples, he too now fears for his life. "How can this be happening?" he asks. A knock is heard and the narrator anxiously hushes the crowd. He then says: "It's Mary. I wonder what she wants?"

In answer, the Deliriou5? song "There Is a Light" plays. The Jesus candle is lit on the word *light*. This time the candle rests not on a red blanket, but on a pure white robe. The first song ends and background music continues as someone reads Matthew 5.

A guide instructs each person to pick up the candle under his or her seat and bring it to be lit by the Jesus candle. From his flame every candle is now lit and the room is filled with light.

With that, the Jesus Journey is over. It's an experience the teens will never forget.

Where now?

What will sermons look like in the future? How will we communicate the message of Jesus Christ to the next generation? And the generation after that? I leave predictions like these to the futurists.

What I do know is that if the Church wants the opportunity to communicate to new generations, we must be willing to change how we tell the old, old story. There is no question in my mind that God is glorified every time we retell that story to new faces.

May God help us to innovate like never before!

The Next Chapter

Experiential Storytelling is just the beginning. You're invited to help write the next chapter! Point your browser to **http://www.experientialstorytelling.com** to explore new ideas, to get additional resources, and to tell the story about how you created your own fourth-dimensional story. The future is waiting to be written.

About the Author

Mark Miller lives just east of the Rock and Roll Hall of Fame in Cleveland, Ohio. Mark is executive pastor at NewSong Church and consults with other churches on reaching postmoderns, creativity, and leadership. He has been a practitioner in ministry for twelve years. He founded the *Reality* youth ministry and is currently pioneering *Journey*, a ministry to postmoderns. He is also the founder of the *Jesus Journey*, an experiential storytelling retreat that makes the story of the Bible accessible to postmoderns. Mark enjoys pushing the envelope and experimenting with new forms of creatively communicating the message of Jesus. And he loves conversing with others who share a similar passion while enjoying a hot cup of cinamochanilla or a plate of Skyline chili (but not at the same time). He has been married to his lifelong friend, Stacey, for more than twelve years and has two beautiful daughters, Raegan and Ramsay.

Bibliography

Cameron, Julie. *The Artist's Way*. New York: G.P. Putnam's Sons, 1992.

Cecil, Brad. "Discerning the Times." *Next* 6 (Winter 2000).

Dyrness, William A. *Visual Faith: Art, Theology, and Worship in Dialogue*. Grand Rapids, Mich.: Baker Books, 2001.

Forbes, Cheryl. *Imagination: Embracing a Theology of Wonder*. Portland, Oreg.: Multnomah Press, 1986.

Hall, Doug. *Jump Start Your Brain*. New York: Warner Books, 1996.

Jensen, Richard A. *Thinking in Story: Preaching in a Post-literate Age*. Lima, Ohio: CSS Publishing, 1994.

McLuhan, Marshall, and Quentin Fiore. *The Medium Is the Message: An Inventory of Effects*. Corte Madera, Calif.: Gingko Press, Inc., 2001.

Miller, Rex. "The Millennial Matrix." *Next* 6 (Winter 2000).

Naisbitt, John, with Nana Naisbitt and Douglas Philips. *High Tech/High Touch: Technology and Our Search for Meaning.* New York: Broadway Books, 1999.

Pellowski, Anne. *The World of Storytelling.* Bronx, NY: H.W. Wilson, 1991.

Pine, B. Joseph II, and James H. Gilmore. *The Experience Economy: Work Is Theatre and Every Business a Stage.* Boston: Harvard Business School Press, 1999.

Reed, Edward S. *The Necessity of Experience.* New Haven, Conn.: Yale University Press, 1996.

Schlossberg, Edwin. *Interactive Excellence: Defining and Developing New Standards for the Twenty-first Century.* New York: The Ballantine Publishing Group, 1998.

Simmons, Annette. *The Story Factor: Inspiration, Influence, and Persuasion Through the Art of Storytelling.* Cambridge, Mass.: Perseus Publishing, 2001.

Sweet, Leonard. *Post-Modern Pilgrims: First Century Passion for 21st Century Church.* Nashville, Tenn.: Broadman & Holman Publishers, 2000.

Von Oech, Roger. *A Kick in the Seat of the Pants.* New York: Harper Perennial, 1986.

Von Oech, Roger. *A Whack on the Side of the Head.* New York: Warner Books, 1990.

Webber, Robert E. *Ancient-Future Faith: Rethinking Evangelicalism for a Postmodern World.* Grand Rapids, Mich.: Baker Books, 1999.

Visual Compliments

to Powerful Ministry

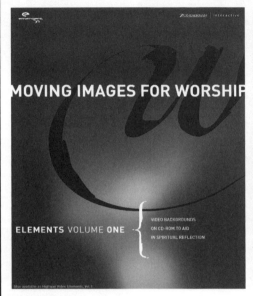

ISBN 0-310-25764-6   ISBN 0-310-25763-8

Themed, video shorts add color, reflection, atmosphere, and emotional reactions that breathe life into your message or worship siutation.

The CD-ROM files will play in most media display engines, suchs as MediaShout, QuickTime, Windows Media Player, PowerPoint, and Real Player, and the .MOV files are completely editable in all editing programs.

Available from **www.emergentYS.com** or visit your local Christian bookstore.

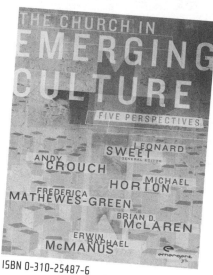

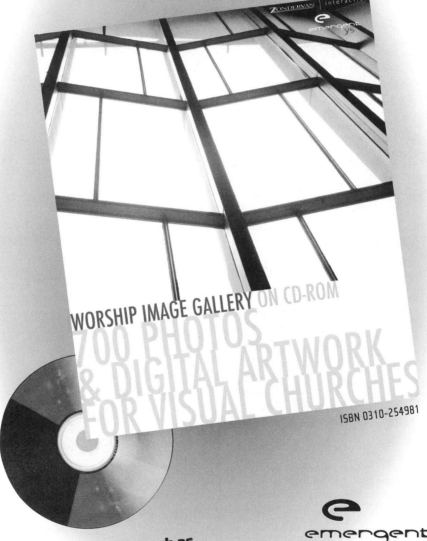

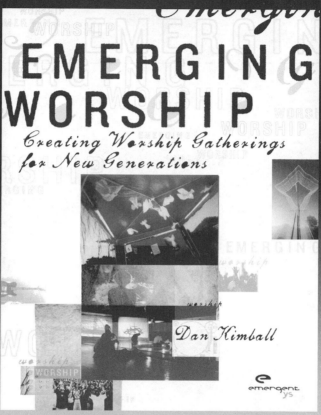